BE ANGRY AT THE SUN
AND OTHER POEMS

BE ANGRY AT THE SUN

ROBINSON JEFFERS

RANDOM HOUSE
NEW YORK

To

DONNAN AND GARTH

NOTE

Six of the shorter poems in this volume were first published in *Poetry*; two each in the *Virginia Quarterly*, the *University Review*, Kansas City, and the *Washington Post*; and one in the *Saturday Review of Literature*.

Due acknowledgments are made; but I wish also to lament the obsession with contemporary history that pins many of these pieces to the calendar, like butterflies to cardboard. Poetry is not private monologue, but I think it is not public speech either; and in general it is the worse for being timely. That is why, for the next-to-latest-written poem of this book, I sought out a drunken fisherman, who lives solitary in his hut under a cliff, and has no radio, no newspaper, no intelligent friends, nothing but fish and whiskey; drugged hermit, his mind should have been as dateless as the ocean. But he too began to babble about public affairs, and I stopped him off.

Yet it is right that a man's views be expressed, though the poetry suffer for it. Poetry should represent the whole mind; if part of the mind is occupied unhappily, so much the worse. And no use postponing the poetry to a time when these storms may have passed, for I think we have but seen a beginning of them; the calm to look for is the calm at the whirlwind's heart.

R. J.

CONTENTS

BE ANGRY AT THE SUN
AND OTHER POEMS

MARA

1

WALKING up from the barn to the house
In the moon cloud-light Ferguson saw a stranger standing
Up the slope on the right: "What do you want?
Hey, you: come here." The intruder paid no attention,
And Ferguson went up to him; the fellow turned—
A man as tall as himself, but backed against
The moon-spot in the cloud it was impossible
To see his face—Ferguson said again,
"What do you want here?" looking up at him, who stood
Higher on the steep slope, and hatefully familiar
Although unknown. The stranger answered in a
　　　　whispering

[3]

Hollow-chested voice like a consumptive's,
"How long will you be satisfied?"—or else, "How long
Will you endure it?"—the words were never exactly
Remembered, for this figure of a man speaking
Receded then, resolved itself into streaks and spots
Of shadow and light on the brown bracken, gray grass
And moon-shot cloud; while Ferguson angry and afraid
Felt his scalp prickle; not superstitious, but angry
At his own senses playing tricks. And that it was true
He could hardly endure. . . What? For he lived the best
Of possible lives for a man of his race, a cattle-driving
And horseback life on his own place, on the free
                    mountains;
And intelligent enough to know it the best;
And married to a beautiful girl, all wants fulfilled: not
                    his own life chiefly
But life in general looked dirty, senseless and destitute
In his dark times. "Christ! What more do I want?
Nothing." The intruder was visible again, he saw its face
Before it vanished. The face was his own.
                                   When he went down
One of his own dogs growled at him, and ran yelping
Into the darkness.

2

A night a year later
He was driving home from Caliente Creek
With an empty horse-trailer behind the car; at Point Sur
    his lights
Picked out three or four cars and a small truck
Parked on the roadside, and a few persons there
Were standing talking; slowing to pass them he
    recognized
Sam Barret's ferretlike face; he stopped and went back.
    "Hello.
Accident?" "Ye'," he said, "the Atlanta." Another man
    said
"It crashed out there." "What's the Atlanta?"—then,
Remembering the name, "The dirigible?" "Ye', the big
    airship."
"Wrecked?" he said. Then a little shaggy old man
Stood up from the bank under the fence, crack-voiced:
"By God, I saw . . ." "Ah, shut up," Barret said.
"He makes me tired." The old man said, "I was here,
    wasn't I?
By God, I saw the mountains reach out their hands
And catch it in the air, like a kid catches a minnow in a
    puddle

[5]

In a dry crick." "Have a drink," Barret said,
Handing a bottle to Ferguson, who wiped its mouth
On his coat-sleeve, drank and returned it: not whiskey
But sick-sweet wine. He felt someone press against him,
Looked down and saw Mary Monahan's young oval face,
   white in the darkness,
And her shining eyes. She felt for his hand, saying, "Oh,
Bruce. Where did you come from?" Then the other man,
Sam Barret's friend: "I wasn't here of course at that time.
I understand from the coast-guard that a bolt of lightning
Broke the ship's back." Barret laughed; Mary Monahan
Said, "That's a coast-guard car: what can they do
Without equipment? They're on the shore." Ferguson
Feeling her nestle against him in the wind and darkness
Bent an arm around her, but looked above her dark head
Across the sand-flat, past the towering black dome of the
   Sur Rock, the glow of the light-house
High on its shoulder, toward the immense gray waste and
   solitude of sea,
The misty light-beam from the rock-height impassively
Circling across it. "How many in the crew?" Sam Barret
   said, "Hell."
His friend said, "Thirty or forty: I guess they're goners."
Ferguson said, "It couldn't lose all its helium;
I think it would float all night. . . . Well,

  [6]

Good night. Good night, Mary." But she followed him,
Walking back toward his car, and said in a moment,
"Bruce. Take me home." "Ah," he said. She said, "That
        weasel-eyes.
They're drunk as bastards. Honey, do you remember the
        night
You and I walked out on the dance at Mill Crick,
And heard the music behind us and the killdeer birds
Crying in the dark?" She sat in the car; Sam Barret
Came alongside and said, "God damn you, Mary,
What's coming off?" Ferguson stood over him. "She's
        going home.
What's that to you?" He said, "Go to hell if you want,"
And went back down the road. Mary said, "Bruce.
Look at the lights." He saw on the vague sea in the north,
        off the dark headland,
A progress of lighted craft, coastguard boats or perhaps
        destroyers, the long beams of their searchlights
Sweeping the water. "Looking for them," he said.
"Well, we can't help." He drove north and the light-line
Stood all along the dark sea, and they passed car after car
        of sightseers,
Who had heard of the wreck by radio and now ran south
With the lit fleet, their idle headlights and the questing
        searchlights

[7]

Drawing coastwise two shining fringes between the long sea
And high black hills.

                At Burnt Mountain Canyon-foot
Ferguson turned up the gorge and up the hill,
And stopped at the Monahan place on the high ridge
Between two canyons. There was no light in the house,
        and the car's lights
Lay over the tops of oak-trees on the empty air
Over black depth. Mary said, "Clyde's in San Francisco.
He won't be home till tomorrow night." Ferguson
Waited in savage contempt of himself and the woman
For the rest of her piece, *stay with me, dear,*
I'm all alone; he switched off the motor and heard
Mary's hands twisting together and a horse moving
Along the fence in the dark. At length he said,
"So you picked up Sam Barret." "You lie," she answered,
And squirmed on the car-seat, pushing her cold face and
        hot mouth
Against his face; his right arm embraced her and his left
        hand
Along the smooth cool thigh under the cloth
Touched the crisp hair, a fraction of his mind thought
"Like a nigger in a dirty story," then Mary Monahan,
Deep-voiced and hoarse: "Oh, God. Stay with me, dear.
I'm all alone." He answered in the doorway

[8]

Of the dark cabin: "Only don't call it love.
The girl I love is five miles from here." "Ah?" she
        answered.
"You fool. Everyone knows she sleeps with your brother
When you're away." Ferguson checked his hand
In the act of striking; he pushed her into the house
And went back to his car.
               Coming home, he fought
His violent need of sneaking to the lighted window
And peek like a dirty spy; he walked back and forth
On the dark path, sweating in the cold air,
And heard the waves beating the gorge-mouth beach
Echo in the mountain. He went in, treading noisily
Up the plank steps and porch.
               Fawn and his mother
Were in the room, Fawn by the table under the lamp
Mending a baby garment, the lamplight stirring
In the tawny storm of her hair; and his mother
Some distance away, sitting erect and still
With her hands folded. Ferguson looked from one to the
        other,
His eyes dazed from the darkness, his tall body
Stooping like a sick eagle's. He said, "Hello, Fawn.
What, you're still up, Mother? It's dark out." Fawn said,
        "Bruce.

[9]

You look so strange: what's happened?" He turned and
        intently
Examined the narrow fastidious beauty of her face,
Puckering his eyes against the lamplight, saying, "What?
        No.
I sold that fox-color mare at my own price.
Not a penny off. Where's Allen?" She breathed and said,
"He went upstairs." "Oh, I don't want him," he answered.
"I think we'll shift the yearlings to the upper pasture
In the morning. How's Dad?" Fawn said, "His pain
Seemed easier today." Old Mrs. Ferguson said,
"He suffers more every day, and it seems wrong
To help him live." "Well, Mother. I know." "A man
        who's ridden all day,
And sinned all night, and never known an hour's sickness
In seventy years." "I guess we all have to catch it
        sometime,
Sooner or later," he answered. "By the way, that dirigible
Balloon of the navy's, the big one you've seen go over here,
Popped and went down tonight in the sea off Point Sur.
People were watching. Nothing ever happens unwatched,
        you know.
What's that to us?"

3

        Fawn awoke before daylight;
The bed was empty beside her, she heard low voices
Through the open window and went and looked down:
        Bruce
And Allen; Bruce mounted already, on the buckskin colt,
Allen not dressed yet, only trousers and boots,
And his shirt in his hand, so that Fawn saw
The beautiful triangle of his back, narrowing
From the shoulders to the loins, warm ivory, the only
Warmth in the world, and she felt herself tremble
So that she dared not call to them. They laughed and
        parted.
Then Fawn called, "Bruce." He raised his long powerful
        face,
That looked like a ship's prow; but being already
Some distance away said nothing, but waved his hand
And rode out of sight up the canyon-side trail
Under the vast dawn-troubled sky and the morning star,
        while Allen
Returned to the house, and in a moment came and lightly
Tapped at Fawn's door. She ran and half opened it:
"Where is he going . . . dearest?" "Why," he said,
        "nothing.

What's the matter, Fawn?" "Conscience. Conscience
        probably," she answered,
"If any." He entered the room; she said, "Don't touch me.
And don't wake Joy," looking toward the small bed
In the dark corner of the room. "What did he say? I know
He . . . thinks about us." Allen said, "Let me tell you
What he was saying. He said you're looking pale
With being too much in the house; he wants you to ride
        again
The way you used to: we're to fetch lunch along
And help him drive up the yearlings." "What is it, a trap?"
She whispered, "Or he'd have waited and ridden with us.
Let me tell you something: there is no snake in all the
        mountain so ugly and treacherous
As you are, Allen. Except me. What has happened to the
        world
To make us liars, cheats and cowards . . . and as hollow
        in here
As dry weed-stalks?" She turned from him to the window
And stood looking out, her slender body and sleep-tossed
        mane
And beautiful bare arms and shoulders dark-outlined
On the rectangular dawn-gleam. He said, "I know.
We're damned, I suppose.

But what else can we do? Wait, wait, we'll manage some
 time
To make this clean. Now get dressed, dear: I'll make a fire
And fetch the horses." He was leaving the room and she
 said,
"You ought to get out of here and never come back.
Only I'd die." She ran and caught him by the arm: "Come
 back.
Ah ah, dear love, forgive me." He, embracing her, felt
With renewed wonder the firm and smooth littleness
Of her sweet body, but when he kissed her she violently
Pushed him off: "You beast let me alone.
If we ... if we ... ever here in this house
I'll kill myself." And again blindly she reached for him
And babbled, "I can't bear ... Oh, Allen, why
Has he done this to us? Maybe he'll come back and kill us
Like coupling rattlesnakes."

>   But he a mile east
Rode toward the pasture, thinking, "Why do I have that
 slimy dream?
Because Clyde Monahan's bitch put it in my mind: but
 why
Was I ready to listen to Monahan's bitch?
Because there've been hints before?

[13]

And spend the night with her: Sam Barret's leavings,
Monahan's bitch? Why: for variety: like an idiot
Pick up a clot of cow-dung being tired of gold.
No wonder the envious droppings
Tried to make pure gold look dirty as herself.
Pure gold? I mean Fawn's natural beauty: there are no
        standards.
How can we say *This is bad, this is good,*
When we know nothing about it, having no standards
Nor faith to judge by? Like flies in a vacuum.
And who will prove that chastity is better than
        commonness,
And for what reason?
Because we've been taught to think so—but who
        taught us?
Tradition: old people: people more ignorant than we,
Away back to the howling tribesmen, the jealous
God and his witch-doctors.

"At least I cancelled the effect, I trust them perfectly.
A man spying on his wife and his brother
Would be too low to live." He smelled the wet delight of
        the dawn-wind
Dropping down the deep canyon to the dark sea, and saw
        the pearl-tender rose-flood

[MARA]

Lining high distant ridges, while still deep night
Slept in the canyon trough, a thousand feet down
Under the shoulder of his horse; he felt a fountain of
        hysterical sadness
Flow up behind his breast-bone through the net of nerves:
    "This is so beautiful:
We are so damned. What good is a man
Living, working, eating, making love, dying,
And leaving a child or two
To live, work, eat and drink, and make love and die,
And so on forever: what good is that?
Either we are animals," he thought, "clever in some ways,
Degenerate in others, and follow instinct,
Or else we are something else and ought to do otherwise.
There's something false in it.
                And if a voice would come
From behind all this . . . color, space, fragrance, power . . .
    we'd not hear,
Or the voice be a liar.
           I shot an eagle once,
And looked at the gorgeous corpse, ruffled the plumes
And saw the lice under them: we the white lice
On this eagle world. I don't make a good louse,
I lack contentment.
One ought to be satisfied with the warm grease

Under the stormy feathers flying through thunder;
Shut eyes and suck."

        He opened a gate and began gathering
His herd toward the high fence-corner, hard work for a
      man
Riding alone; his mount had a lathered hide,
Bloody flanks, trembling knees, after an hour
On that steep range. Ferguson let it breathe a little,
And, looking down the long cataract of rock-set ridges and
      their blue shadows pouring to sea-level
From the new-risen sun, saw Fawn and Allen,
Small, clear and distant, riding up from the west
Along the lip of the canyon, above the blue mist and
      hollow shadow
That brimmed its gorge.

4

        The end of August the air
Grew dry and anxious, there were forest fires inland
And the grass was like gunpowder. Old Andy Ferguson
Lay sick toward death in the long attic room
Under the roof of the house; his glazed blue eyes
Blinked at the rafters, his hand under the bed-cover

Continually stroked his pain, isle of dull fire
In the dry flesh. By his bedside the little radio that Allen
   had given him,
With a two-armed wind-wheel to feed the battery,
Prattled unheard. The old man, still a rancher
Though bed-fast, sick and drug-dazed, sniffed the dry air
And twisted his head about on the pillow, peering
At the gable windows; there was danger in the south,
And the sun shone too red. He reached down by the
   bedside
And scrabbled with bony fingers until he found
A smooth stone cylinder, pestle of an Indian mortar
He had plowed up on the place, and now it was used
For a call-bell: he hammered the floor with it ,
Until his wife came upstairs; tall, thin, cold in that heat,
Pale, with gray hair and rust-brown eyes. "Yes, Andrew.
What can I do?" He, handling the lump of pain:
"Where's"—his mind lost his son's name—"Akh," he said,
   "*he—*
The tall one—Bruce?" "I haven't seen him," she
   answered;
And he sharply: "Which way is the wind?" "The wind?
I haven't been out this morning." "Open that window."
She went and opened it; no wind came from the south,
But copper sunlight. "I can't see any fire, Andrew,

Only smoke. Shall I call Allen?" "Call what's her name . . .
His wife. She's got more sense." Mrs. Ferguson
Sighed sharply and said, "*Bruce's* wife; Fawn McDonald.
Must I call her?" She called from the stairhead, but her
      thin voice
Found no one, and she went down.

                    Fawn came upstairs,
Barefoot, bare-throated and bare-armed for the heat,
Naked in a scant dress, her yellow-brown mane
Appeared the biggest part of her. The old man: "Ha,
Y' look like a tadpole," laughing feebly in the dream-fringe
Of his pain and its opiate. "I'm scared of fire this weather.
Any damn' fool driving along the coast-road
Can drop a light." She said, "There's fire just south,
Working up Marble Creek; you can hear it crackle,
But there's no wind." She laid her hand on his sweating
      forehead;
His face a wet yellow skull, except the grizzle
Of a week's beard, and the still powerful jaw-muscles
Deepening the open graves under the cheek-bones,
But he was Allen's and Bruce's father. "I'll watch,"
She said, ". . . Father." He said, "I can stand pain:
I can't stand lying here like a trapped rat.
Every man has his rat-trap and this is mine.
Hell, we'll have music." He reached out his lean arm

And switched on the full power of the radio, which had
      changed tune
And been muttering unnoticed: now a passionate voice
Barking a foreign language beat through the room under
      the sounding-box
Of the steep roof, bringing no meaning but emotion,
Scorn and dog wrath, cored on the wailing of a lost child,
To this far shore. Old Ferguson snapped it silent
And said, "What's that?" She said, "Hitler, I guess.
They're starting a war." The old man said, "Shit," and
      wearily
Handled his pain; spurred boots were heard on the stair,
And Bruce's voice: "Y' might 'a' let me wash first, Mother.
Ah, not a scratch. Forget it." Fawn paled and cried out
When he came in: he was blacked with fire, but what she
      saw
Was the fresh crimson on his hands and shirt: "Oh . . ."
      she moaned,
And her voice hushed, "*What have you done?*" He
      impatiently:
"You too? It's nothing, nothing, horse's blood." He
      looked at his father
And suddenly turned back on Fawn, intently examining
Her lifted face: his lined and smoke-etched, and the sharp
      black

Pupils prying through the pale eyes frightened her. He
      said,
"*What did you think I had done?*" She stammered, "No.
Hurt yourself," turning her face toward the window. He
      rather tenderly
Turned it back to him, she felt the sticky thumb-print
Staining her chin; then his eyes let her go.
He spoke to the bed: "Well, Dad?" "You been fighting
      fire.
Is it bad?" "No," he said. "Fight? It's going away from us,
It'll pinch out on the south fork o' the creek.
I just came through it." The old man wearily handled his
      pain
And said, "What's all the ketchup for?" Then Fawn was
      conscious
That Allen stood in the doorway behind his mother;
She dared not look at him. Bruce said, "The poor colt,
The poor bastard. A what y' call it, mercy-murder.
I'd nothing but my old knife and the artery
Sprayed like a fire-hose." He continued, awkward and
      ashamed:
"Well, Mother, I couldn't sleep: I rode up Marble Ridge
And saw some queer things or dreamed 'em. I came down
      in the morning
And met the brush-fire; liefer than go ten miles

Around over the mountain I put the colt through it.
He could 'a' jumped it easily but he went crazy
And fell, and got his knees burnt to the bones.
I brought the saddle home." The old man mourned,
 "That buckskin?
A hundred and fifty dollars gone to the vultures.
We mortgaged the place t' give you an education
And set up Allen in business: have y' cleared it any? You
 both came home
Empty as tin cans." Bruce said, "I'm sorry, Dad."
The old man: "All right, all right. All this doctoring
Costs more than a colt; we're even. This dirty pain-killer
That doesn't work."

5

 Fawn took her little daughter and went down
Into the canyon to bathe where the slack stream
Made a green pool; the sheer cliff of the gorge
Closes it on one side, and alder and thick-growing
Laurel on the other. Here were cool sand, smooth rock,
Rich moss and the water music; while the ebb-tide ocean
In the autumn heat stank like a beast, and high overhead
 the flayed gray ridges harsh as flint knives
Flamed in the sun: Fawn knelt in the pool, soaping

The thick fleece of her hair; when she bent to rinse it
The bow of her back and her small buttocks beautifully
Arched from the stream, her mane like rich water-weed
Floated in the green ripple; and she stood up,
Her knees were red and white with the pressure of pebbles
Under cool water; while little Joy, fourteen
Months old, played on the bank; she too enfranchised
Of her cloth shell, the animal loveliness
Of their naked bodies was bud and flower
O' the rose-white lily: they were nearly as beautiful as a
        young panther
With her soft cub: but Fawn a somewhat degenerate
        animal
Craving love more than giving it had not been able
To suckle her baby: she had small virgin breasts,
And now recovered from childbirth her smooth belly
Looked virgin too. She stroked herself with her hands
Lovingly, stroking the water off; she dressed herself
In one garment, and took the child and went up
To sit on a hot stone and shake her bright hair
Dry in the sun.

        From here high above the storm-warped
Spires of the redwoods in the rock throat of the canyon one
        saw the concrete

Rainbow of the coast-road bridge; now and then a car
Ran across it like a bead on a wire; beyond it the huge and
        turquoise ocean naked of mist
Lay like a rock. Hundreds of yellow butterflies
Drifted up from the shore, and Fawn sat thinking
Of the dance tonight. She heard a crash far away down the
        mountain
And saw a cream-colored car go through the bridge-head
Guard-rails, and rather slowly sidewise pitch
Into the canyon. There was nothing to do about it
At this distance.

6

        Old Mrs. Ferguson had undressed
But wakeful sat erect in the stiff chair
By the ill-burning lamp, lean and hieratic
In her flannel nightgown. A weekly newspaper
Lay on the long flat lap unopened; the woman
Stared straight ahead of her at the wall of the room,
Seeing nothing but through the window with the eye's
        corner the flashes
Of heat-lightning on the sea, flash after flash
Like an unsteady pulse. She heard the dry wind

Rattle the house and heard little Joy her grandchild
Crying; and the dogs barked at the lightning.
She felt the house emptiness; they had all gone
To enjoy themselves. The old woman pursed her thin lips
And fell to remembering the time, twenty years ago . . .
        twenty-five years . . .
When her own little Gordie died of pneumonia.
Bruce was four years old then, Allen not born yet.
The rain poured night and day and the wind raged
And the child fought for breath. There was no one to
        fetch a doctor;
Andrew being out with that loose woman who later
Died of consumption.
And there was that evil woman Teresita Blaine;
And all the drinking and card-playing . . . "He is being
        punished for them now.
Well, I forgive him.
        He really was Gordie's murderer.
Oh, poor little blue lips begging for breath,
Your father killed you.
        And once he allowed that evil
Beast Teresita Blaine to come and insult me
In my own house.
I was happy when the boys were little, I was happy then
In spite of all.

He trained the boys to corruption,
And Bruce has married a loose woman . . . Fawn . . . Fawn,
Her fancy name, and they go off to a dance
Because this is her birthday, leaving me here
To take care of her baby and a dying man,
And think about that wicked harlot Teresita Blaine, whom
      I hate so,
Wherever she is. *He* did this to me. I was young and
      happy,
And always a faithful wife." The heat-lightning flickered
      wildly, and thunder
Over the house-roof. Thunder? No: that old man
Hammering for attendance, pounding the floor
With his stone tool.
        Old Mrs. Ferguson sighed
And went upstairs carrying the lamp; its light
Shone upward on her flat breast and corded throat;
She stood by his bedside: "Do you want something,
      Andrew?
What do you want, dear?" (This is that great lover.
Do you want Teresita Blaine or what other woman,
You breathing corpse?) "I am in pain and that baby
Crying all the time, what's the matter with her?
Gi' me another shot o' the medicine, Sarah.
Put me to sleep." She stood and looked down at him

With helpless pity and arthritic hatred, the frequent
　　　　ultimates
Of long-lived marriage; she answered, "The child is
　　　　spoiled
And must cry it out. Her pretty mother is away
Enjoying herself." He was silent, then pled with her:
　　　　"Listen, Sally.
Gi' me another shot o' the medicine.
There's red-hot rats in my belly crawling and biting."
　　　　She wiped his wet forehead
With a corner of the sheet, then sat by the bed
Holding his speckled old hand; stroking it, pressing it
Against her cheek.
　　　　　　Out of these, Lord—
A cancerous old man, a jealous
Wife nightlong reciting
Her litany of ancient wrongs,
And a little young hot adulteress
Between her two men—out of these ordinary
Elements of common life, these two or three persons
Who not without cause question it,
Can any discovery shine, or a hawk rise?
For you are not human, no respecter of persons,
Nor subject to disgust nor a stickler at sin,
And your ways are all beautiful.

Even your decaying things, the sea-slime and carrion
Shine in the dark; even this troublesome decaying time
That does evil in its dreams,
Drunk with treacheries and cruelties,
Phosphorescent with wars,
Flares like a torch.
It has its own forlorn honor, and its pillars of music
To the pure stars.

7

        Fawn Ferguson whispered: "Don't
Dance with me any more, Allen, I'm scared.
His eyes are queer and he keeps watching us.
I think he's drinking too much." Allen said, "Well,
Let him watch us"; but Fawn slipped from his hands
When they passed the open doorway where Bruce was
        standing.
She said, "It's too hot," and to Bruce: "Let's go outside.
You're right not dancing, it's hot.
How it smells in here," the air rank with bad perfume
And fume from the lamps and lanterns. Bruce smiled
        down at her
Through the chopped waves of guitar-music and said,
        "What?
I couldn't hear you." She said, "Let's go outside.

It smells in here." He seeing at the moment Mary
        Monahan
Moon her dark eyes toward him, twisting her maenad
Body in Ed Flood's arms: "Uh: sweating cowhands
And inflamed women.
Maybe we need a war: but you know I feel as if
They were my brothers and sisters." Fawn in amazement
Stared up at him: Bruce professing brotherhood with
        people? His face looked blind
And high like a ship's prow, cleaving the crowd
To the outer door. Then she saw Allen dancing
A little too close for courtesy with Brenna Morgan,
Her blood-red-enamelled mouth and black hair: he'd not
        been long
Finding a substitute!
                The night out-doors was feverish
        with silent lightning and a hot wind,
Dry weed-stalks and waste paper scurried from the south
        like rabbits across the dark foreland, and a gang
        of horses
Rushed aimlessly back and forth, stamping and squealing.
        The sky was black, and the ocean, but its foam
        shone
Phosphorescent between the lightnings; and a few drops
Of rain fell suddenly.

So here the night: far eastward began
the day and the war; the dazed eyes of ten
million conscripts
Watched its bleak morning, and the blunt-nosed
bombing-planes roared over Poland; the great
catastrophe
That involves many little ones had found its landing-
field.
Bruce Ferguson
Walked in the dark and saw the quarter-century-
abandoned
Lumber-mill on the cliff's edge, its humped-up roof-line
And crazily tilted iron smokestack
Black on the distant lightning-sheet, he felt his mind
Clutch that clear form, as a man climbing a precipice
Clutches a horn of hard rock, "This will not flow
Out of my hand." He found himself for a lightning
moment
Outside the flux and whirl of things, observing the world
From a fixed point. He saw the small spinning planet,
Spotted with white at the poles and dull red wars
Branding both cheeks, and the sun and the other stars like
herds of wild horses
On the vast field, but all vanished with the lightning
Before he had time to think of it; then he perceived

[29]

That Fawn had left him. He went back toward the light-
        haze
Flung from the wide door of the dance-hall, but stopped
And went around under the shining windows
Toward the rear door, the bar-room. "I won't look for her.
        Am I a dog
Watching his meat?"

                But Fawn, where they were dancing,
Stood alone by the wall and watched Allen
With Brenna Morgan, thinking, "Tall, coarse, black-
        haired,
And sweats under the arms: is that what he wants
Next after me?" The dance ended; then Red O'Neil,
A wide-shouldered young man with a broad face,
Reputed the best dancer on the Coast, except
Allen perhaps—he came to her and said, "Dance,
Mrs. Ferguson?" "No," she said. He said, "Drink?"
She looked for Allen and missed him, and said, "How
        wonderful,"
Lifting the word in her clear voice like a lark to heaven,
"How did you know?"

              In the bar-room she felt
Bruce his high head and pale eyes instantly aware of her

And then withdrawn. She thought, "Not Allen but
       another man,
What's his name, Red O'Neil for a red herring,
That's good," and chattered, "Isn't it like earthquake
       weather?
It makes my hair stand up." "Beautiful," he said,
"I can't keep my hands off it." She felt with loathing
His strong blunt hand, and for some female reason
Nestled her head against it—hard stubby fingers,
They were like a strangler's—and flattered him with
       sidelong eyes.
He said, "I thought you'd green eyes." "Aren't they?"
       "No, blue.
Wi' li'l gold stars in 'em."

                Toward midnight the heat-lightnings
Had ceased to flicker, and a real thunder-storm
Broke the equivocal tension of the air. It bellowed in the
       south,
And a fierce wind through the cracks of the old building
Made the lamps flare; then jagged lightning
Leaped overhead, the outer night for an instant
Far brighter than the lit room flamed through its windows
And wide doorway, and the following thunder like a black
       cloth

[31]

Covered the dance-music. Rain mixed with hail was heard
And ceased; and the dance changed; for Johnny
Garcia, the fiddler, excited with storm and whiskey,
His instrument squealed like a caught rabbit for the next
   flash,
And sobbed in the pause, until the roaring black cloth
Covered it; and he marched up from the folds of thunder
Like one who has triumphed over death. The guitar-
   players, the two
Vargas brothers, watched him and caught his mind,
But the dance wried. There were women afraid of thunder,
And men too drunk to dance, and the difficult music
Subdued others; only Allen Ferguson with his new
   partner,
A straw-haired thin-armed girl in a green dress,
And Red O'Neil with Fawn Ferguson remained dancing;
   and the lightning flared, the fiddle
Screamed like an eagle, the thunder choked it. In the
   triumph afterwards
Allen reached out his arms to Fawn and she came; he
   tossed his pale
Partner to O'Neil. She was tired and hung in his arms,
But Fawn was like a Thracian bacchante, wanton-eyed,
   reckless with pleasure, her body pressed

Against Allen's, her lips panting, her head flung back
Lolling on the taut throat, shaking the brindled meteor
Of lion-color hair.
                Bruce came from the doorway,
Walking awkwardly and blindly like a sleepwalker
And self-consciously smiling. His head and shoulders
Were wet with sleet. He passed by Fawn and Allen,
And took O'Neil by the shoulder and said hoarsely,
"No more. No more." O'Neil said "What's the matter
          with you?"
Attempting to jerk away from him; and the girl whined,
Seeing Bruce's face. O'Neil let her go and said,
"Now, you drunk. What?" Bruce said heavily, "Ah,
          listen to me.
I won't . . ." The rest was not heard, for thunder pealed
And the mountain echoed it. The two men faced each
          other,
Waiting on it for a silence; Bruce shook his head
Like a dog shaking the noise off and said heavily,
"This girl's too young. I've seen. I've stood there. I have
         been patient.
Oh, I could name some women here"—
He looked for Mary Monahan and failed to find her—
"That are nature's own stretched whores: dance with 'em.

[33]

But this girl's pure, she's innocent. Put up your hands.
I'm going to smash you." O'Neil grinned and flashed
A fist like a snake's head into Ferguson's belly, and one to
        the face
When it gasped and came forward; then the men closed,
Wrestling, they were well matched, both powerful,
        O'Neil
Thicker and shorter. They looked ridiculous and pitiful,
As men do when they fight without weapons, the human
        body
Being essentially unwarlike, nor fang nor talon
To enrich its poor wraths; and Fawn kept moaning
"Oh God, how funny," watching with enormous eyes
In a shrunken chalk face; while the three musicians
Still worked their instruments, nodding their heads,
        watching but drugged
With their own music.
        Ed Flood, Clyde Monahan, Sam Barret
Drew in on the fighters, to part them or to take sides, but
        Ferguson
Already had hooked his left arm around O'Neil's neck,
And with the other fist hammered his face
Awhile, and dropped him. O'Neil on hands and knees
Stupidly watched the blood splash on the floor,
The others stood back a step, then Ferguson still

[34]

Snapping and gasping stammered at them, "Anyone
       here . . .
Ha . . . Anyone think this red-haired pimp
Didn't need fixing?" They were silent; the fiddle
Screamed softly for a weak lightning-flash. Fawn moaned,
       "Oh, Oh,"
Watching the blood fall; Allen gray-faced and sick
Came to his brother, knowing *whose* debt O'Neil
Had paid a penny on, but willing to back the creditor
At need. But there was no more to do. Bruce sighed,
Stroked his long face with his hand, and said hoarsely,
"Well, we'll go home." He looked around and saw Fawn,
And stood watching her while the receding thunder
Roared along the shore northward, her pure pale face
And staring eyes under the mane of hair the smoky
Lamplight discolored. The noise ended, he went to her,
Still walking like a sleepwalker, and she in terror
Watched them make way for him. He stooped over her:
      "I'm sorry, little one.
Made a fool o' myself. Ah, to hell with it.
It's nothing." There was a festivity of Chinese lanterns
Strung at this end of the room, and Bruce suddenly
Reached up over Fawn's head and plucked one, tore the
      bright paper
And took the candle; and another; he gave them to Fawn,

One in each hand, while her mouth made a smile,
And her fear-hollowed eyes questioned him, and the hot
      grease
Trickled on her trembling hands.
                          Sam Barret and some others
Were helping Red O'Neil to the wash-room; they stopped
In the doorway and stared. Bruce said: "Little one:
Your birthday. Twenty years old: do you want twenty
      candles?
Oh, two's enough: hold them high, Madonna." He
      couldn't imagine
Why the Italian word came to his tongue:
"Madonna, you're beautiful enough to pray to.
And so young. But if . . ." He stood and gazed at her,
And she held the two candle-stubs. He said, "Oh, if.
If that which is not true were true I'd kill.
By God, I'd kill." She looked straight in his pale
Eyes and saw leaping insanity there, and said steadily,
"I know you would." "Well . . ." he stood stroking his long
Bony hands together in the Pilate gesture. "Bosh," he said,
"Come, we'll go home."
                    He took her by the arm and led her
Slowly across the dance-floor, sixty eyes watching,
And Fawn not daring to drop the candles felt the hot wax

Cake on her hands. Bruce led her carefully clear
Of the blood on the floor; then Allen who had followed
Came up beside her, she between her two men
Passed through the door. There was no wind, the candles
Burned in the outer night all the way to the car;
When its lights were switched on she dropped them.
                Bruce made her sit
On the front seat and said to Allen, "You drive,"
And left them there. Allen went after him and took his
        arm,
Felt the hard muscle jerk, and said, "Where you going?
Come *this* way." Bruce kept on walking. Allen said,
        "Listen,
Bruce: come on back." Bruce kept on walking; then Fawn
Left the car and followed them. Bruce said, "Take her
        home.
Get out of here." Allen said "Bruce . . ." Bruce stopped
And turned on him: "I'm not coming, you fool, let go.
I need to walk." Allen said, "You're crazy. What,
        fourteen miles?"
Fawn stood in the dark at a little distance, trembling and
        picking
The skins of wax from her hands. Allen said, "All right.
Then I'll walk too." Fawn picked at the skins of wax.

[37]

Bruce said, "I'm walking alone: get to hell out of here.

Damn you, don't you think I trust you with her? What's
        the matter with you?

She wouldn't look at you." Allen said, "Sure. I know it.

Come on home, Bruce." Fawn picked at the wax and said,
        "Allen.

Watch out." But Bruce did not strike, but turned and
        strode

Into the darkness. Allen stood still; when Fawn

Went back to the car he followed her.

                      Neither of them spoke;

They watched the light-track along the road for Bruce,

But never saw him. Near Gavilan Canyon bridge Fawn
        said, "He's crazy.

Insane." Allen made no answer. "Insane and dangerous:
        I thought he'd kill you." "No," Allen said.
        Fawn said,

"He said he'd kill." The road dipped toward the sea and
        the headlight beams a moment overlay the
        lonely

Incessant waters piling and playing by themselves among
        their tide-rocks. Fawn said, "Take me away,

Allen. We've got to." He was silent, and said,

"What do you mean?" She said, "We've got to. Tonight.

That would be clean and decent, if we go away. This life
        is false, dirty and vicious, and I think
Ends in a horror.
Like their foul war will." Allen made no answer. Fawn
        said, "It would save us.
It might save Bruce." Allen drove slowly and said,
"You mean you'll stop and get Joy . . ." "No.
I will not stop. Let him keep her; it might help him. Your
        mother'll see to her." He said, "Clothes?" "No.
Nothing. We'll leave the car in Monterey. I will take
        nothing." At Hurricane Point, where the road
Is cut in a rifted mountain and every winter the rock-slides
        close it, Allen said,
"How will we live?" "*I* don't know. People live."
He said, "Can you live without little Joy?" "Yes."
"And you can do this to Bruce. Well: *I* can't." "No,"
        she answered,
"You can sneak and cheat. You can nibble off his piece
        when he isn't looking.
You can make love a rotten thing." He said carefully,
"Keep your nerve, Fawn." She instantly began to scream,
As if he had touched a spring in her, knife after knife
Of glassy noise, he unheard stubbornly saying, "We must
        not destroy

[39]

Him nor ourselves." Near home, on the high shelf
Under Marble Ridge foot he was driving fast, suddenly
    the car
Yawed to the precipice edge and back to brush
The rock-cut bank, while the rubber of the tires
Screamed on the road-bed: then the cramp wheels were
    righted,
And the locked brakes released. Fawn said, "Why didn't
    you
Go on over, you coward?" "Sorry," he answered;
"Deer crossing the road. We'd 've had venison
And a smashed car. Did y' see their green eyes?" She said,
    "For God's sake
Get me safe home."

8

    Bruce walked the road, and cars
Coming from the dance passed him, he moved to the
    road's edge
Each time the light-streak flared, but never thought of
    them
Until one stopped. It said, "Ride?" "No," he said, and
    heard it

Whispering to itself, then laughing soprano
Like a drunken woman. He said, "Get out of here," and it
        drove on.
The mountains, those were *real* persons, head beyond
        head, ridge, peak and dome
High dark on the gray sky; and the dark gullies and gorges
        and the rock hearts . . . slightly tortured . . .
The raw sore of this road cut in their feet:
The slow anger of the coast mountains: they'll get their
        own back
After some time. Things will be better then.
Rock-slides will choke the road, no one will open it.
You dark young mountains are going up in the world, we
        the people going down. Why? Because
Nobody knows the difference between right and wrong.
So the wolves will come back to Europe. Here, poor
        people,
Slower we rot. It's a pity she's pure:
If she went to bed with him I could kill her,
And, oh, the peace.
        He turned on someone walking beside him:
"What do *you* want?" She in a soft slurred voice
No more syllabic than the ocean's: "I have been here for
        years

[41]

At the locked doors of your mind knocking . . ." "Go on,"
     he said,
"I'll believe anything." She said, "You used to want to
     understand,
You used to want to know the truth about things,
And whether all this . . . immense establishment of earth
     and stars,
Flesh, mind and time and so forth has any purpose.
But now you are lost in passion." "Hm? Not a bit. Passion?
Cold as a fish. If I weren't . . .
Who are you, anyway?" "Mara," she answered, but when
He looked at her she was gone, and it seemed to him
That he'd been talking to himself. "Mm. Mara. If it's got
     a name,
What does that mean?
If I begin to hear voices and see visions . . . Ah?
A filthy symptom. Hold myself tight in hand,
Not think too much, and be cold as a snake. But she was
     right:
Living's not good enough without knowing. Who knows
Anything? So living's not good enough. So we slog on,
Blind, blind and blind."
               He had a continual sense
Of someone following behind him and rapid steps
Close on his own, but turn as quickly as he might,

He never saw her. Home before dawn he found
The old house in the mountain darkness awake and
   staring
From many windows. The door stood open; a chair
Lay overturned on the floor, and the place was vacant
But lamps burning. Upstairs in the dark hallway
He saw his mother's door underlined with light, he opened
   it a crack:
"Are you awake?" There was no one; the bed
Was in disorder, and a drained lamp burned low
On the chest of drawers. Ferguson looked over his
   shoulder and said, "Well, Mara,
My quiet companion?
The old man won't be gone, anyway." Going up in the
   dark
To the attic room he heard Fawn's voice from the stair-
   head,
"Oh, Bruce: is that you?" and saw her leaning dark
In the sudden light of the doorway. He made no answer,
   she stood aside for him
And followed him in.
      The usual morbid odor in the room
Moved his compassion, but his father's hollow jaw and
   closed face
Seemed out of pain. His mother sat stiff erect

[43]

On the chair by the bedside, blue pale and panting,
With narrow defiant eyes; her flannel night-dress was torn
From the bony shoulder, one long flat breast hung bare,
Poor empty purse, long drained; and she had the dignity
Of a great queen. Allen stood near her. Bruce
Stared and said: "What?" Fawn murmured, "Oh, awful."
     Allen said,
"She was running down to the sea and I had to catch her,
     she fought me.
The old man's dead." "Oh," Bruce said. He stroked his
     hand
Wearily across his eyes: "You know it's much better for
     him, Mother,
Why grieve for that?" She moved her lips without speak-
     ing, locked them again,
And sat rigidly erect. Allen said, "On the cliff.
I had to carry her all the way back.
I tried to put her to bed but she came up here.
She thinks she killed him." Bruce said, "You loved him,
     Mother, you cared for him faithfully, to the end.
Now come: lie down and rest. You can rest now. You
     wouldn't want him to go on living,
The way he's been." The old woman looked at him,
     shuttering her eyes, then looked at Fawn

And said, "You whore." Who gasped and stepped back,
        and Allen
Came in front of her. Bruce stood like a dead pine-tree,
        high, stiff and brittle, bark and branches all
        fallen
From the gray spire: he looked to the left, where there was
        no one, and said,
"Stop laughing." Allen said, "Mother . . . Mother, for
        God's sake,
What does that mean?" "And you," she said, "dancing
All night while I and your father labored in hell.
Let them hang me, I loathe life." And to Bruce: "I was
        worn out taking care of him; hating and pitying.
I poured out his month's medicine into two glasses and
        made him drink it all.
I forced him, I beat him down. My will was stronger than
        his. I'd been his . . . thing, I cringed to him so
        long . . .
But at last I was stronger. See? Heh, the pitiful old fool:
        we made a game of it,
I called it whiskey." Bruce said dully, "You couldn't bear
Seeing him suffer." "He was still breathing," Allen said,
"Slower and slower. We couldn't do anything.
Then she ran down to the sea." Bruce said slowly:

"Why did you call her that name, Mother? Is there . . .
        something I ought to know? Hm? You can tell
        me.
I won't do anything." Fawn said suddenly and clearly,
        "Kill me, Bruce,
If you think such things of me." The old woman answered,
        "You can tell by the mouth.
She looks exactly like that evil beast Teresita Blaine, who
        took my husband and insulted me
In my own house." Bruce groaned and said wearily,
        "What? Oh, that?
I've heard you speak of it.
But this is *now*. Curious how we can hold
Smoking bits of hell in our minds for a hundred years.
        Trifles, but hot. Now, Mother,
We have to plan. My mind feels very clear this morning
For some reason."
        He glanced at Mara; she was still
        standing there,
And that troubled him a little, knowing her to be
Not a real person in any common sense of the word,
But yet she stood there; and curiously enough his father
        was near her,
Or a smoky semblance of the old man, erect, half smiling,
        looking down

At his own corpse. He thought quite possibly
The old man's spirit was there indeed, one hears of such
       things, but Mara
Is a different sort.
            He unglued his eyes and mind
From both his phantoms, painfully, for the purpose and
       meaning of things
Seemed rather in that world than this. "Mother." He took
       her hand
And gripped it, to catch her mind with a little pain.
"Can you hear me?
You didn't give him the stuff. You didn't give it to him.
You left the bottle by his bed, and the poor old man
In bitter pain or perhaps wanting to die took it all
In your absence. Understand? That is the story.
I mean the truth: Mara and Allen can swear to it
If necessary. But no one will ask; for he was dying
In any case; and those who have this disease
Are always in simple Christian mercy sent out of the world
In a drug-poisoned sleep. Mm . . . I think you'll find great
       peace
Now that it's done. Come down to bed, Mother,
And think no more of it. Dream about roses, Mother.
You've always wanted a little garden, now you'll have time.
I and Allen will attend to things."

9

Allen alone

Accompanied the old man's body when it was taken
To Salinas for cremation. He returned after dark,
Haggard for sleep; Fawn heard the car and met him at
      the door:
"Was it . . . all right, Allen?" He nodded: "No trouble.
Here?" "Quiet," she said, " . . . restless: they and their
      ghosts
Walking all over the house: I think she's sleeping now.
      Kiss me,
For God's sake, Allen." She felt the paper-wrapped
      sharp-edged
Metal box in his hand: "What's that, dear? . . . Oh,
I know." "Mm," he said, "this little size, this little
      sediment. Live seventy years
And be a boxful of bone-ash." "Oh God, Allen,
Why do you look at me as if you hate me?
When shall we live?" They moved guiltily apart and
      Bruce
Came up the path, a pail of milk in one hand
And a lantern in the other. He stood in silence, then
      Fawn anxiously:
"There was no trouble, it's finished," and Allen said,
"I just got home." "I saw you," he said, and to Fawn:

"Well, are you glad he's back?" She breathed and said,
        "What?
Certainly." He said, "Yes . . . ah . . . by the way, Fawn,
Will you boil the milk before you feed Joy? I noticed
A string of blood in it. I think not a disease,
I think my hand was too hard, but boil it." Fawn felt a
        climbing
Spasm in her throat. "I'll remember." They made a
        strange,
Beautiful and secret group, the upward light gilding jaws
        and cheek-bones,
The night-bound island of lantern-light against the dark
        house-wall, and the mountain overhanging
Like a black wave. Bruce said, "Mm . . . I, have . . . been . . .
        thinking.
The old man's death kind o' pulled me up.
I want to tell you . . ." He hesitated and said fiercely,
        "Forgive me, will you,
For a vile and insane error of judgment: my mind must
        'a' been
Clear off its hinges. Let that pass. By the way, Fawn,
Will you boil the milk before you feed Joy? I noticed
A string of blood in it." Fawn said, "I heard you. . . .
        Bruce?
What did you mean?" Hah?" he said. She obstinately:

[49]

"What do you want forgiveness for?" He said, "You fool,
Let that corpse float. It's deadly and it stinks.
Ah . . . everything was all right, Allen? Of course.
Now we'll be quiet . . . you know, quiet, quietness. God,
       how we'll sleep."

10

Fawn lay in bed, clenching her little fists,
Watching a red half moon like a burning ship
Founder on the sea-rim; she heard Bruce moving in the
       attic room
Where the old man used to be, and heard through the
       open window the melancholy roaring of
       sea-lions
In the off-shore kelp: Bruce had come in half an hour ago
After being gone all day, no one knew where,
And she and Allen in lonely beds ached for each other
But were lovers no more: therefore her pillow
And cheek and hair were so wet.
                          Let them be. She got up,
Climbed the attic stair in the dark, and stilly opened
The stairhead door. Bruce was hunched over a book, like
       a hawk
Killing a rabbit; the smoky lamp by his shoulder

Haloed him with dull light, the long room was cavernous
Dark under the ship's-keel roof. Fawn stared and said:
"Dear? May I come?" "What?" he said, "Why not?" and
            closed the book,
Keeping his finger in the pages. Fawn said, "I can't sleep,"
And came nearer the light, hoping he'd notice
That she'd been crying. "Why do you hate me, Bruce?
Why do you leave me lonely the days and nights?
What have I done?" "Hm?" he said. "No. Nothing.
            Reading here,
And switch on the news at midnight." "News," she
            answered,
"Dirty and bloody and what does it matter anyway?
May I stay here?" She smiled at him and sat on the bed,
The stripped mattress. He said "Uh . . . listen, Fawn.
As you say: blood, lies and dirt, imbecility and rottenness
Is the news.
And if we look into our hearts—uh?—the same hell's broth.
All that's good's crippled; every bad thing
Has big hands and strong heart and wings like a hawk.
            Well,
I don't understand this, I want to study it." Fawn stared
            at him,
Feeling extraordinary contempt
Behind her level eyes and sweet oval mask,

[51]

And said, "What were you reading, dear?" "What?" he
        said, "A book.
I got it in college, I never read it."
He switched on the radio and said, "A German professor
Who thinks this bloody and tortured slave called history
Has regular habits. Waves, you know, wave-lengths,
        separate waves of civilization
Up and down like the sea's; and the same sort of . . . life,
        arts, politics and so forth
At the same level on each wave, you can predict 'em.
        At present
We're on the down-rip." Fawn heard him dimly through
        a stopped tune
And the chatter of the radio-announcer as the hour
        changed,
And, naturally, understood nothing nor cared to,
But she saw his excitement.
                There were now three parallel
        currents of human action in that high cavern
Closed by a film of shingles from the cloudy stars. There
        was the bodiless voice of the news-caster
Palely reflecting far-off agonies, as of Poland killed,
        massacre in China, ships and men
Drowning in death-cold darkness in the North Sea; and
        there was Ferguson's

Voice weaving through this curtain of woes: "The little
        professor
Wrote thirty years ago, he was quite a prophet, he's dead
        now. If the whole Western world's on the skids,
Explains each person, uh?
I wish to God I had some religion." He paced back and
        forth
Under the inverted valley of the roof, the lamplight
        making odd work in the eaves-corners with his
        shadow,
And thought, "Not if it's lies or delusion, like all of them
Up to this moment. I want the truth. The truth.
Even if it poisons us or makes beasts of us"—while Fawn
Drew up her legs on the mattress his father had died on,
        and thought, "Allen
Won't touch me now. Allen's scared. This one's only crazy,
And he's the better of the two, stronger and decenter and
        more a man,
Except in one way,
And my husband. Oh, Allen, Allen. Good-bye the
        ecstasies,
Perhaps it was only terror that made us passionate.
Crazy with natural jealousy, but I can cure that." She let
        the night-dress
Slide up her body, baring the beautiful legs

[53]

And flank to the cold night, "If I can make him love me
    now
We'll be all right. Dear God, I want to be safe again,
Happy again. Not happy: tranquil, decent, at peace. I
    want to be good.
That's all, that's all."
The radio had left its tragic theme and was gabbling
Baseball scores; Bruce thought, "A star gives light,
So does a burning city full of dead bodies, Warsaw
    burning's no worse than Arcturus burning,
And adultery's as good as honor. Fool, still harp on that?
She's pure as crystal. So what of it? A Tibetan woman
Will marry a whole flight of brothers and be honorable
In fact and reputation, the esteemed wife
Of four at once, it's all in the country custom,
Nothing in nature." Fawn, cold and mostly naked,
Cuddled herself like a kitten on the bed: "Darling:
I'm so cold; let's go down." He shut off the radio
And thought, "I wonder what the poor dupes in Poland
Think about promises now, egged on to fight
And left to die? Decline of the west: decline and fall's
Moral first, the rest follows. Morality's rooted
In religion, religion's hypnotic lies,
When you wake up you're lost. Ah? All but Germany.
They'll hold together awhile, for they've got a hypnotist,

Sort of *ersatz* one . . ." Fawn sighed and came to him
And pressed her body against him: "Feel how I'm
        shivering.
Let me get warm against you, take me in your arms.
Dear, I'm so cold." He patiently: "What is it—cold?
        Go to bed, child,
Or get some clothes on." She through her clicking teeth:
"Good night, good night," and went down the stair,
        and past
Old Mrs. Ferguson's door to Allen's, which she opened
Neither noisily nor carefully. She closed the door
And tried to lock it, the slot in the sagging frame
Refused the bolt and she left them. She knelt by the bed
Like a doll praying; but before Allen's nerves
Gathered themselves to speak she fled back again
To her own place.
              Bruce in the attic room lay down after while
On the stripped mattress and slept. In his dream he felt a
        stench and decay of corpses everywhere,
So that he refused to breathe, and watched along the
        reddish horizon of his dream twilight the huge
Blade and tumor of a wave to come and wash clean. It
        came, it was not water but blood,
It caught him with empty lungs because he'd refused to
        breathe; he awoke strangling

[55]

And lay and panted like a thirsty dog. Every night its
        nightmares. He slept and dreamed again.
Fawn came in with her throat cut like a cake: every night
        its nightmares:
Better not sleep.
          He went down, carrying the lamp.
There was a gray walker in the passage and his mother's
        voice:
"Bruce . . ." "Ah," he said, "what?" She said, "I hate life."
"What, Mother, can't you sleep either?" "I am a woman
Who ought to be drowned or hanged, he and you stopped
        me.
Go in and look at him." Bruce remained silent, and said
Slowly, "Well there are two of us can't sleep, but why
Wake up another?" "*Two* others," she said, "wake up two
        others.
She's in there with him." The fish-tail flame of the lamp
In Bruce's hand flicked up a smoke-thread and steadied,
        then regularly trembling
Wrote a small oval orbit on the house darkness, while he
        answered
Coldly, "You are mistaken. We all have nightmares.
Go back to bed.
We all have dreams, Mother, we have to distinguish
Dreams from reality. Well, it can soon be proved,

If that will make you feel better." He went to his brother's
Door, and his hand disobeying his mind flung it wide so
        violently
That it threw back on the wall and the noise crashed
All through the house. Instantly his mother screamed,
        "I've hated her
From the first day I saw her. Now she's caught. Ah, Ah,
        Ah, Teresita Blaine
Come out, come out." Allen sitting up in bed
Blinked and shuddered in the light; Bruce said, "Brother,
You're lucky tonight."
He turned fiercely on his mother: "Look. Look your eyes
        out.
Do you see that it's empty? Get down, look under it.
What, no one? Peer in the slop-pail: perhaps your
        personal devil Teresita Blaine is in swimming
        there
In the soiled water. Agh. . . . Forgive me, Mother.
We love you: I hate your jealousies. This is the sink-hole.
This is the pit: you and I, dirty spies,
Mole, ant and lizard tower up over us like giants:
This is what we call degradation: and jealousy
Is the way down to it.—She had a dream, Allen.
Take care of her. I'm going out."

11

There were two women
Cadging for nickels to play a slot-machine.
One of them came to Ferguson and said, "Honey,
Are you as cross as you look?" He gazed a moment
At her weak eyes, red mouth and boneless face,
Fairly pretty but bloated, then without answering
Looked over her head and past a half dozen drinkers
To the sunlit door of the bar-room, and Monterey Bay
sparkling with light, where a hundred
fishing-boats
Lay at their moorings and the long curve of beach
Fainted in a bright haze; a V-formation of pelicans was
flighting over; and there was something
Sinister, cheap and malignant in so much sunlight: this
little whore,
Poor thing, was cleaner. He said, "Are you sick?"
"What?" she said.
He touched her cheek: "Bloated, bloated. What a pity.
You were beautiful before you drowned." She opened her
mouth
To curse, but remembered the green money she'd seen
The cattle-buyer paying him: "What's the matter,
darling?

[58]

Are you so lonesome?" "Uh?" he said. "No. Thinking of
       Finland,
That brave race, and they haven't a chance.
Courage is the only value left in the world:
It must be crushed: it must go through the rock-crusher
Along with the old stones from Sinai.—Drunk," he
       thought, "making
Speeches to a tart. It might be called degradation. Oh,
       well,
There are deeper wells." She sidled her flank to his:
"I guess you think too much, honey."
                            He looked over her head
(Pleasant waves of brown hair, but that's done in shops)
       through the open door
At the sun-smitten bay, and saw as clear as reality
Huge points come up through it, higher than the masts of
       the purse-seiners, the polished tines
Of enormous antlers; the horny beams of the antlers
Broke water; the boats pitched and rolled over, sea
       foamed; the head
Of a mountain-size elk came out of the sea and the
       wrecked fishing-fleet
Poured from his shoulders. The great split hooves pawed
       the shoal water; a whirlwind of gulls
Screamed by the hocks.

    [59]

               Ferguson knew perfectly
That all was imaginary and only his mind
Making a picture of crazy violence: perhaps it wanted
Violence? "There's plenty of that in the world: and you
Will work out your case quietly." He looked at the
           woman's
Trivial fat face; she sidled closer to him and said,
"I'm thirsty, dear." He said, "That's the salt sea.
I never slept with a drowned woman: what d' y' charge
On the sea-weed bed under the little swimming fishes?"
           She patiently:
"I wish I could do it for nothing, darling.
I got to live." "Yea? Go away and live then." She looked
To the bar-man for sympathy, and finding none
Floated away. Ferguson said, "Wrap me up a pint,
I'm going."
           But as he went to the door
He heard choked laughter; several people he knew
Were sitting at one of the little tables watching him,
Whispering and giggling. Red O'Neil was one. Ferguson's
Wandering eyes, weary with liquor and lack of sleep,
           instantly
Stilled and flared, like a hawk's.
                    He went to their table

And said, "I did you some wrong a few months ago,
Red. I was wrong." O'Neil had pushed back his chair,
And stood, not knowing what might happen. Sam Barret
       sat grinning,
Clyde Monahan looked at the table, Mary Monahan
Made eyes like moons: "Darling! We never see you any
       more.
We saw your car outside and came in to look for you."
       Sam Barret
Giggled aloud, Mary mooned her dark eyes at him and
       said to Ferguson:
"Who's your fascinating friend?" "A woman . . . *like you*,"
He said carefully. Clyde looked up and said nothing;
Ferguson turned to go out; Red O'Neil said,
"Go on to hell." Ferguson turned a stone face
That looked perfectly controlled, except the abnormal
       pupils, glassed-over coal-pits
In the pale slits; O'Neil stepping backward from them
       tipped his chair over, but Ferguson
Said nor did nothing, but turned again and went out
With Mary's laughter on his back.
                   He found on the driver
Seat of his car a note scrawled with red lipstick
On the blank side of an advertising hand-bill:

"Darling, ask your darling wife who she meets
In the shack on Mine Crick. Maybe you know." His
        unfocused eyes
Worked up and down the blurred limbs of the letters:
They seemed too big to read: and the apes watching, he
        heard them
Tittering along the sidewalk: but if he went back
He might in a bull rage kill the wrong person again. He
        fumbled his pocket
For his clasp-knife and opened the four-inch blade; the
        apes
Backed into doorways; he folded the paper carefully
And sliced it to shreds along the creases. "Be careful, be
        careful.
Never let go; be careful. . . . Is the gear in neutral?
Now press the starter. Now shift. Shift again. Drive
        cautiously.
Hurt not a fly till its guilt's proved. What's guilt or
        innocence?
Conventions, no more; dying and rotting conventions.
My mother the murderess,
My sister the whore,
What are they cooking up
Behind the pantry door? Cookolding up.
And they are all innocent, all innocent.

The poor man lost one eye peeping through keyholes
And the other in the war, but, dear God, give him proof,
He'll do what hell requires. Hell? This is hell,
I'm driving through it, the dirty larvas and imagoes
In mummy-cases lining the road like a row of fence-posts,
Fire to their knees."
He passed the pinewood and fantastic Carmel village and
   the artichoke fields; sea-fog was licking
The lordly feet of the coast mountains; and a drive of
   steers on the sea-road their horns and rolling
   eyes meant something
Obscenely evil: he worked the car through them
And thought, "Whose herd? I never saw this herd before,
   nor the Mex drivers." He ran his car
Into the bank near home and went up to the house; they
   were sitting
At the noon meal; he stood in the doorway, his mother's
   wiry eyes estimating him, and Fawn's
Terror-struck, sideling; she had been cutting the baby's
   meat on her plate, and, though December,
   slow flies
Vultured the table. Allen stood up and said, "Are y' hurt?"
   "Uh?" he said,
Stooping tall in the doorway like a stilted heron
Over a stream, "Fawn will you come outside?

I want to talk to you." She gripped with both hands her
        chair-seat edges,
And sighed, and her teeth chattered. Allen said, "Bruce . . .
What's the blood?" For he'd slashed his hand slicing that
        paper
And had not felt it; hands, face and clothes were smeared,
The little artery still oozing: now he saw the stains:
"What have I done? . . . What was I going to do?"
And turned and went out.
                Going down the hill he saw very clearly
Two images in his mind: the one of Fawn dead
With a sliced throat, the other of himself self-hanged,
And he must choose. Naturally a decent person,
He chose the second and hung by a horse-hair hackamore
Under a beam in the barn.
                He will now no longer
Bawl for the truth, the truth, though it were poisonous,
Nor feel two thousand years of instruction sag underfoot
Like a rotted floor. Nor will he feel the wind,
Nor taste the rain, nor see again the great crowning beauty
        of the year, that southeast storm
In the week of Christmas or New Year's, when the wind
        tugs the roof like a righteous man
Lifting his unfaithful wife by the hair

[64]

[MARA]

From the bed to the door, and under a roaring blue-black
        sky the black
Ocean flames all over with flying white foam,
And no bird flies. Nor will Ferguson look up
At two gulls flying over the branding-fire in the April
        evening
On the knee of the mountain. The young grass is crushed
        and blood-laked,
The calves bawl, the men are tired and brutal, whiskey is
        drunk,
And in the bluish twilight two scythe-wing gulls
Drift over the reddening beauty of the fire,
Mewing, and stretch down their necks: then someone
        looks up
And feels a strange thought. It will not be Ferguson. Nor
        will Ferguson
Hear news of widening wars and deepening disaster,
Nor of the great retreat from truth, and the moral
        confusions
Deeper confounded. Did he imagine time could stand
        still?
The cause is far beyond good and evil,
Men fight and their cause is not the cause.
There are no angels and no devils,

[65]

Christ unopposed would corrupt all.

There was a vast and lovely sundown that evening, soft fire
   and roses,
Wine, amber and honey to the heart of heaven, and
   the sea
Glassed it with long reflections. Three herons flew over.
   Fawn had wept a little,
But now she stood with Allen on the hill by the house,
Her little perfect face glowing in the light,
And said: "We mustn't blame ourselves, dear, too much.
He was insane. If we had not been lovers
He would have been insane for some other reason.
I'm sorry for him.
Well, dear, he has given us freedom and happiness."

12

This pallid comet announces more than kings' deaths.
To tail it with purer color I add
That the mountains are alive. They crouch like great cats
   watching
Our comic and mouse-hole tragedies, or lift high over
   them
Peaks like sacred torches, pale-flaming rock.

[MARA]

The old blue dragon breathes at their feet, the eternal
        flames
Burn in the sky. The spirit that flickers and hurts in
        humanity
Shines brighter from better lamps; but from all shines.
Look to it: prepare for the long winter: spring is far off.

THE BOWL OF BLOOD

*The scene is: On the left, the interior of a fisherman's cabin;
on the right, low shore, dark sea and sky, waning red spot of
sunset. Perhaps a dead tree, so that the Maskers may hang
their cloaks on the stubs of its boughs.*

*A poorly dressed middle-aged woman is lighting a lamp in
the cabin. The Maskers, three cloaked and hooded figures,
are outside in the twilight.*

FIRST MASKER. I do not know whether it is possible to pre-
sent contemporary things in the shape of eternity.
SECOND. If it were, it would please no one. The present is
always a crisis; people want a partisan cry, not judgment.
No long views, for God's sake.
THIRD [*to First*].
You have that far-off look again. What do you see?
FIRST.   I? Groveling hawks.
Wounded hawks fighting to death on a cage floor
Very ignobly, the great wings beating not the blue air
But blood and excrement. And you?

[68]

THIRD.   I see this hut,

And the woman in it, between the muddy North Sea, cold,
    shallow and dark, where men are dying,

And the dark marsh. This place is northward of the Elbe,
    the Schleswig shore. In peace-time there would
    be lights

On the islands, but the beacons of Europe are dying.

SECOND.

I found a small yellow flower on the marsh,

How does a flower dare?

Pitiful thing, its petals blackened with frost.

Look, the first flower.

THIRD.   Yes, it is April.

Here the snow has melted, but in Norway

Red blood on the snow.

In Finland has the snow melted? Not yet.

The blood on the snow has blackened; in Poland the
    blood,

Black lies the blood under white snow,

Black lies the blood.

FIRST MASKER.

How can one man gather all power?

How does a man dare?

This is an evil thing, too dark to understand,

What meat fed Caesar.

SECOND.   Yet I can answer you.

Listen: power is a great hollow spirit

That needs a center.

It chooses one man almost at random

And clouds him and clots around him and it possesses him.

Listen: the man does not have power,

Power has the man.

THIRD MASKER.

That man you speak of, who wears for his cloak and
           weapon a mighty nation, is even now

Coming here along the track through the swamp.

Look, you know him even in this blinkard owl-light, his
           face is famous. What brings him here?

This is no central place, no field-headquarters nor capital
           city, this is the mud-draggled

Tail of the earth; and he comes not with power nor armies
           but two companions, and not with confidence

But seeking counsel. Stand back, watch awhile.

[*They stand rigidly motionless, against the curtain of sea
and sky. The Leader enters, followed by Von Steinfurth
and Colonel Weiss, and stops outside the cabin.*]

THE LEADER. What? This beachcomber hut?

STEINFURTH. Yes, sir. The woman is very poor. She takes no
presents, and I should say that guarantees her honesty.

THE LEADER. I am not one to scorn poverty. However . . .
  back to the car.

STEINFURTH. At your orders.

THE LEADER. Wait. I have the Air-Marshal's word for her
  talent, as well as yours and Weiss's, what?

WEISS. It is almost unbelievable, sir. He was most deeply
  moved. We know now that the dead live; we know they
  can help us with their counsel and their knowledge.

THE LEADER. Sceptic I am still. Hermann and his Karen, ha?
  Go in: announce yourselves.

Leave me alone a moment to gather my mind,

And wash it in the North Sea, under the Wagnerian

Ruins of that sunfall.

WEISS. At your orders. [*He and Von Steinfurth knock and go
  in.*] Evening, Frau Gertrud.

THE WOMAN. Come in. Where is the gentleman?

STEINFURTH. He is just outside. Are you ready?

THE WOMAN. Will you help me move this bench? There will
  be not more than three of you? [*They arrange bench, chair
  and so forth.*]

THE LEADER [*outside, alone except the Maskers, who are in-
  visible to him.*] Ach. I hate gambling.

I hate gambling with German lives. Those murdered
  troopships: five thousand men choked in the
  Skaggerak

[71]

Because I moved. Well, I was forced: you have to win
      wars or lose them. Win, no expense
Has been too great, the luck of a thousand years hangs
      on it.
Lose, there is no possible estimation of the hell to follow.
      I believe in victory. I
Believe. I believe. I will believe.
I believe . . . in eventual victory, but *this* throw's lost, it is
      hopeless now to hold Norway;
And all the dawn-feeling dies. Therefore I've come
To a wise-woman: ach, say it: a solitude-crazed
Fishwife for prophecies. [*He turns and stares at the sea.*]
FIRST MASKER. This is the man whose finger-ring
Is greater than the girdle of any king.
THIRD MASKER. He is looking at his last enemy,
The heavy corpse-laden corpse-cold sea.
THE LEADER. Empty, dark, death-cold. Not a hint
Of all the secret, violent and prowling life out there, mine-
      sweepers, mine-layers, transports, cargo-boats,
Our death-giver steel fish lying in their courses, and the
      cruisers, the damned English destroyers, all
      watching,
Watching, watching, watching. The night rank with eyes
      and nothing shows. Somewhere out yonder

[72]

Heligoland keeps his sacred watch.

And over the sea in the northwest the accursed harbor
      Scapa Flow, where our navy

Broke its bright sword. Beautiful dead ships, you will be
      avenged.

SECOND MASKER. He has fine dreams, not altogether free
      from nightmare.

FIRST. You have great dreams, sir.

THIRD. You never make a mistake, never make a mistake.

FIRST. With sleepwalker certitude . . .

SECOND. One step at a time you climb up the ladder.

THIRD. The Rhineland. Austria. Bohemia. These are great
      steps.

FIRST. Poland. Denmark. Norway.

SECOND. Conqueror, these are great steps . . .

THIRD. To fall from . . .

THE LEADER. Unbearable! [*He strides to the cabin door and
goes in, leaving the door open. He stands just inside the
doorway.*] I must never be alone now. While I was in
prison my thoughts were good angels, they were my bless-
edness, my daily nourishment. Now that I stand near the
peak of the world—biting devils. [*He turns up his cloak-
collar, concealing the lower part of his face.*] Ha, Steinfurth? Have you raised any ghosts yet?

[73]

STEINFURTH. We are ready, sir.

WEISS. This is the woman, sir. Frau Gertrud, this is the gentleman who wishes to use your power.

THE WOMAN. Yes. [*To the Leader*] Who are you?

WEISS. He is Mr.... Maximus. A man of highest importance, an important . . . steel-manufacturer.

THE WOMAN. So you told me, but it does not matter. Well, noble sir: if you are ready? [*She sits in the arm-chair, bending forward over a basinful of dark stuff that has been set on a stool before it.*]

THE LEADER [*disturbed, indicating the basin*]. What is that?

STEINFURTH. Only blood, sir. It is not aesthetic but it is necessary. It is her method.

THE LEADER. That I don't like. I won't have it.

STEINFURTH. No show without it, sir: she inhales the vapor and drifts into her trance. It is only swine's blood . . .

THE LEADER. I hate blood. The good liquor should stay where it belongs. Well . . . go on, go on!

WEISS. Sh. We have to keep silence, sir.

THE LEADER [*loudly*]. How does one direct the affair, call the spirit one wants?

WEISS. By thought. You must think of those whom you wish to meet. Our thought calls them.

[*The woman breathes convulsively, leaning over the basin,*

[74]

*then stiffens back in her chair. Some of the light shifts to
the outdoor side of the scene.*]

FIRST MASKER. The great man wishes to see the spirit of
some dead person.

SECOND. Do the dead live or not? Life is a masker.
Certainly the dead live, but higher and faster
Than living people.

THIRD. Faster? This corpse-floating sea
Lives, and has changed very little since it began to be.
And the rocks live, grain by grain dropping masks from
         their almost eternity.
Earth and sky live.

SECOND.   And when man, woman or child
Dies, it is only someone dropping a mask.
A little personality lost, and the wild
Beauty of the world resumed.

THIRD.   Why did you ask?
It is only the on and off of a mask.

FIRST MASKER. Very well. A mask can be peeled off, a mask
can be put on again. [*He throws off cloak and hood and appears in an old blue and red uniform, adjusts mask and
peruque.*] I am Frederick the Great, who laid in sweat and
blood the foundation stones of the German Reich. [*He
goes through the cabin door and appears within, at first
dimly, then clearly.*]

[75]

WEISS. Ah . . . look!

[*The Leader stands up, with some appearance of agita-
tion.*]

FREDERICK (*rather disdainfully*). Je suis le roi de Prusse. Et
vous qui m'appelez en aide: qu'est-ce que vous êtes?

STEINFURTH [*whispering*]. Sir: the great Frederick!

THE LEADER. Silence. I understood. [*To Frederick*] You were
the king of Prussia. I am the chief and Leader of the Prus-
sians and all other Germans, north, south, east and west.

FREDERICK. Their Leader . . . toward what? At the worst I
had always England for my friend. What have you done
to England . . . Austrian?

THE LEADER. I hoped . . . I planned . . . Oh, I was patient.
But they hate us.

SECOND MASKER. [*outside the door*]. The interview is not
coming off well. We must give him another counsellor.

THE LEADER. Now I shall crush, crush, crush England.

Ha? Not I but your own blood and successor,

The old outcast at Doorn burnt the roast.

He bungled them into hating us: mend it could no man.

Where am I leading the Germans, King? From ruin to
            dominion.

From degradation and poverty to honor, wealth, power,

Vengeance and victory.

FREDERICK [*shrugging*]. Hm. Vengeance. Rache . . . .

revanche . . . This damned human race. [*He turns and goes out.*]

THE LEADER. Wait! Give me a sign . . . Did you see his thin evil smile? He hates me: all hate me.

[*Outside the cabin door, Second Masker takes off cloak and hood while first resumes them. Second, entering the light in the cabin, wears the mask and attitude of Napoleon.*]

SECOND MASKER. I rode the storm and subdued my enemies. I am Napoleon.

THE LEADER. Ach . . . no!

NAPOLEON. The eagles perched on my wrist. I would have unified all Europe.

THE LEADER [*waving his hands in aversion*]. Begone! You failed, you failed, you are ominous.

[*The Masker goes out, and resumes cloak and hood.*]

THE LEADER. A man who embroiled himself in Russia before he had settled with the English: what madness! That mistake I shall not commit. And there will be no St. Helena for me, while my finger can twitch a trigger.

Lord God, what is it in me, what worm in the brain, what
        mental traitor

Keeps whispering, "You too must fail?" After all that hope
        and faith, the labor, the long preparation, the . . .
        crimes . . .

[77]

Blood, terror, treacheries in a just cause . . . no, one can't
      fail. Die, worm.

This brain's too tough. It is for final disaster and the ruin
      of Germany

That God or fate or luck has preserved my life through a
      thousand perils and raised me up, up,

To supreme power. Which I foresaw ten years beforehand
      and was not deluded. That at least's proved,

That future. But, Oh dear God, let me know the rest, and
      kill myself

If it is bad. Save what's possible for Germany and kill myself
Before the fall.

This is my Gethsemane night, Christ's agony in the
      garden: only to great artists

Come these dark hours. [*He sits down, his head in his
hands. Light shifts to the Maskers, outside the cabin.*]

FIRST MASKER.

It is necessary from time to time
To turn the eyes away from mankind,
Frederick the Great's "verdammte Rasse,"
Or be choked with pity and laughter.

SECOND.

The posturings, not the wickedness;
The poverty, not the excess.
Whoever thinks this man is more wicked

Than other men knows not himself.

THIRD.

If man must always have man in his eyes and nostrils
Mass-suicide perhaps might be best.

FIRST.

I will contemplate the high mountains
Far south of here.
Over each peak pale stand the stars,
Blue the alpine night.
Look, the rocks are like tongues of flame.
Each mountain is more massive than a nation of men,
And gracefuller than any maiden.
Pure hangs the snow.

THIRD.

If man must always have man in his eyes and nostrils
Mass-suicide would be his best hope.

SECOND.

I will contemplate the high ocean
Far west of here.
Hard blows the wind, headed with spray
High run the waves.
Look, there is not one man
Nor work of man to be seen in all this rich world.
Red in the foam hang the westering
Feathers of day's end.

THIRD.

If man must always have man in his eyes and nostrils

Mass-suicide would be his best savior.

FIRST. Meanwhile, the Leader is having his dark hour.

SECOND [*coming forward*]. Before we proceed with the poem, I should like to point out to our friends here that even Hitler, though all too mischievously occupied with human affairs, does have a sense of the other world, the inhuman one. This North Sea sunset that has just gone west; and the Berchtesgaden landscape, the nature-dreams of Wagner and so forth. It is romantic, therefore incompletely effective, but still it is one source of his power. If it were effective it would lead to a crisp refusal of that kind of power, but of course it is merely romantic and makes him suffer.

FIRST. You mean that he is slightly a poet.

THIRD. So are those with him. They say "blood and soil," while the West says "democracy." Did you ever hear a prosier word? Democracy: the clay life-belt that sank Athens, and is sinking France. Blood and soil are poetry, you can fight for them; democracy is pure prose, abstract, indefinite, and, as they use it, dishonest. Why can't the West cry "Freedom"? Words have great power, and the world is changing.

SECOND. Freedom a definite word?

THIRD. No, half prose: abstract but noble. It is comparative:
as for instance, the Englishman has more freedom than
the German, and the German than the Russian; but it is
a word that poetry can accept and men can fight for.

FIRST. Proceed with the poem.

THIRD. Did I forget it? [*He turns and speaks through the*
cabin door.] Leader: you had a friend once . . .

THE LEADER. I had a friend. It sticks in my mind that I had a
friend once . . . Lord God, not Roehm.

Not that one. Yet if he came and stood here, blood-
   splatched and shame-stained, I'd tell him to his
   face he got his earnings,

He needn't gnash at me.

THIRD. You had a friend once . . . Friedenau . . . remember
Ernst Friedenau?

THE LEADER.

I had a dear comrade when I was young.

The heart is warm then, that grows abstract and bitter
   with ripeness; and we were comrades in the
   great war,

The constant shadow of death sharpens friendship. Like a
   lamp, faint by day, clear and warm at night. . . .
   Erich? Erich?

Was that his name?

THIRD.   Ernst.

[81]

THE LEADER.   Surely in a moment
I'll remember him; I loved him well. He was blond as
                  Balder, and brave and true. He was a poet,
And felt the future. He said we'd lose the great war: I used
                  to curse him for that: but still he prophesied
German re-birth.
He fed my flame, he taught me much, then he was killed.
I was sick in the hospital, nearly blind . . . Ernst . . .
                  Friedenau . . . can you come to me?
Whether you wander the world of light or moulder cold
                  in the long grave-trench, come to me, comrade,
It is growing gray here. I need you; my faith is sick. I have
                  lost confidence.
That lost, all's lost.

[*Third Masker throws off his cloak, enters the cabin as Friedenau, a young German soldier of 1917.*]

FRIEDENAU. I am here.

THE LEADER.   Ernst! Is it you? How the light shines!
Tell me what I must do. I have terrible responsibilities to
                  bear, and am like a man
Lost in a fog.

FRIEDENAU. Ah, go on, go on, go on through. What else can
                  you do?

THE LEADER.   Listen, Ernst.

We have crushed Poland. First I compromised a sick
        peace with Russia, and . . .

FRIEDENAU. My dear Addi!

We know all that.

THE LEADER. You used to feel the form and pressure of fu-
        ture events: what must I do

Now? Wounded: an eagle: we've clapped one wing over
        Denmark and one on Norway, but the right's torn.

Ach, can we never win one fight on the water?

Broken, I think.

FRIEDENAU. You'll hold Norway.

THE LEADER.   What? I hope and doubt. We
        have Oslo by a miracle,

But the English in the north . . .

FRIEDENAU.   You'll howk them out.

THE LEADER.   How
        can that be, with enemy warships off every fjord

Holding the sea, pouring in new forces?

FRIEDENAU.   You'll howk them
        out again.

THE LEADER.   Lord God, can I hope again?

How soon?

FRIEDENAU. This month.

THE LEADER.   Don't mock me, don't trick me,
        Ernst. We were friends once.

FRIEDENAU. Still friends, I hope. Yet you are using me, as you
do everyone.

You haven't even asked whether I am happy or wretched.

THE LEADER. What . . . ach! Are you well, Ernst? Is it well
with you?

FRIEDENAU.

I am a crier of incredible victories. I say your generals have
planned to the last millimetre

Times, means, fields, roads, but Brauchitsch's youngest
most hopeful staff-officer

Hardly dares dream the truth, that two months from now

France will have fallen.

THE LEADER. Ah, yes? Is that all? . . . I do not believe you,
Ernst. I'll believe you can flit about and peer over people's
shoulders, and have been reading one of those lightning-
war time-tables and taken it literally. I myself know that
there are always impediments, mistakes, failures, something overlooked. Plans go through or . . . crash . . . but
not on schedule.

FRIEDENAU. Remember me sixty days from now.

I see the huge tides of iron and fire, roaring wings and
violence, tricks and treacheries, rehearsed and
invincible,

Scour Holland, Flanders, and France, river and canal,

fortress, flood, field, broken armies. I see your
war-engines
Rip the enemy front to ribbons, like screaming flesh under
a meat-mincer, I see the poplar-lined roads
Packed with fugitives, your planes rake them from the air,
your heartless machines crush them in ditches, I
see, I see . . . What is that
Innumerable flock of lost sheep wandering
At Dunkirk on the wide glassy and shelterless beach?
The broken British army, horror in their eyes,
Looking for rowboats . . . While at Sedan the steel and
stone shell of France cracks like a filbert-shell,
And the battle is finished and the world changes: your
Mediterranean jackal, timid and fierce,
Bites the feet of the fallen: leave a few morsels for him.
Tell him to feed his white teeth in Africa
While you take England.

THE LEADER.   England too?

FRIEDENAU.   What could stop you?
The English army is lost, driven into the sea, and all the
coasts of Europe to launch from.

THE LEADER.   By God
Is this the truth?

FRIEDENAU.   Knot up the tally sixty days from now,

[85]

And ride on the neck of Europe. Ah? *But*, world-
        conqueror,
One word of warning: strike not England too soon.
Prepare first, prepare. Make new plans. Manage France.
        Breathe the armies, rest the air-arm. Wait for
        September.
The battle will be grim and bloody, multiform, monstrous,
        unimaginable. The victory is yours.
Strike in September; or if later, better.
[*Light shifts to the right of the scene, where the First and
Second Maskers stand against the dark sea.*]

FIRST MASKER. You heard him say "September."

SECOND. "Or later." Why does he give false advice?

FIRST. Because a prompt invasion would catch England in
anguish and end the war this year; which is not intended.
The war must grind on, and grind small. It must not end
when France falls, nor when England is beaten. It must
not end when the ends of the earth are drawn in. God is
less humane than Hitler, and has larger views.

SECOND.
    And a liar like Hitler?

FIRST.   God's spokesmen are often liars.
God remains silent.

SECOND.   And I writhe
Under the knives.

I have heard a story about freedom, a vain vain tale
Told by some Greeks, by some slave-holding Greeks
And a few Roman authors, Rome being the greatest
Slave-driver in the world before Spain and Britain.
Freedom's a costly luxury.

FIRST.   I've heard that the Swiss,
Being poor and warlike, each man his mountain,
Won and maintained freedom.

SECOND.   Look at Switzerland,
Civilized now.

FIRST.   Then civilization?

SECOND.   Its ripening
Is freedom's crisis. Men must keep in their minds
The one way to be free: that's to be better armed
And stronger than others, and not covet their goods,
And stay frugally at home, death to invaders: the Greek
                states flowered
While this was theirs.

FIRST.   And now the world piles up
Into continental masses?

SECOND.   Freedom must wait.
This is the hour of masses and masters. There's no free
                man
But the anachronistic little lord of a herd on the hill
And a few horses.

FIRST.   What? Would you fight for that?

SECOND.

Until I died. For freedom and a piece of land
Who would not fight to the death?

FIRST.   Death is that thing.

Death is the great argument that keeps my mind
Wild in the wind.

[*They throw off their cloaks to appear in black tights with
white bones painted on them, and skull masks. They
dance, to a clack-clack rhythm, the old Totentanz.*]

SECOND. Then wander in Warsaw.

FIRST. I'll walk in Rotterdam.

SECOND. Lordly and loud

FIRST. Leap over London.

SECOND. Give me Berlin.

FIRST. Capering in Coventry, calling our comrades . . .

SECOND. Berlin, Hamburg, Bremen, Emden, Duesseldorf,
                    Mannheim . . . Like a hawk on Hamburg . . .

FIRST. Sea-slug slimy I swim the sea-lanes,

Swift as a shark, shearing the sky,

SECOND. Diving through clouds death keeps carnival,

FIRST. Hunger and horror hosting behind him. . . .

SECOND. Like a hawk on Hamburg . . . how do you rhyme
                    these things?

I'll lie on Berlin like a lion on his lair,

[88]

Havoc on Hamburg, fire-hail on Mannheim . . .

Kiel and Kieff, Naples and Helsinki . . .

Give me Europe.

FIRST. Misery to millions, captivity, massacre . . .

How many years?

SECOND.   I want Europe.

FIRST.   One year? Two years?

SECOND [*wheedling*]. Give me Europe.

FIRST.   Ten years? Twenty years?

SECOND [*imperiously*].   Count not the years!

Give me Europe.

FIRST.   Europe is yours. [*They stand rigidly still.*]

SECOND. It was only the taking off of a mask.

[*The light shifts again.*]

THE LEADER.

My God, what are those voices?

FRIEDENAU.   Nothing: spirits of the air:

Pay no attention.

THE LEADER. *I did not want this war.* [*Anguished gesture*
    of washing hands.]

Innocent. Innocent. They forced me.

I was aimed eastward and they knew it. Could I take the
    Ukraine

While Poland and Czechoslovakia were enemy wolves

[89]

Flanking the bear's den? But Britain was jealous and
  France afraid, and Jewry
Worked its black magic. Ach, that pious old smiler:
The old man understood me well enough, he knew, *he
  knew*
What we agreed at Munich though no one spoke of it—
And he went home and slipped me into war:
Chamberlain the smiling moneyed man, Daladier
The scared career-man, Churchill the bloody-minded
  amateur,
Roosevelt and his playboy envoys whispering them on:
  Lord God! Lord God!
Bring down my enemies, the wreckers of Europe.

FRIEDENAU.   You must not listen
To those disturbing voices, only to victory.
[*First and Second Maskers dance again.*]

FIRST MASKER.

Have you fallen in the sea, my Leader?
So stained your clothing, and drips,
Drips. Are the dark stains
Fuel-oil from sunk ships?
Blood are the stains,
And the water is tears.

SECOND.

Oh, yes, they all share the guilt,

All the governments, all the great nations stand
With blood on their hands,
And the long course will run,
But what victor will assess the war-guilt again?
Dance you dead bones.

FIRST.

My Leader, play out the tragedy,
Down into dreary revolution and despair,
Exhaustion and shabby horrors and squalid slavery,
The Russian theme. What is it whirling in the air,
What is it eddying up from the ground
All over Europe and around
The whole planet, like the dim poisonous air
From the split rock under the Sibyl's roost?
What is it whispering and lifting like autumn leaves
Or desert dust or spray blown from high seas?
Hatred, pain and despair,
Valid curses, vain prayers,
Revolt and torture and the wailing of women.
Dance you dead bones.

SECOND.

I will go up to the high mountains, my Leader,
And try not to remember that the best youth of England
          and Germany, the boys without blemish,
Have passioned in the air and fallen in the pit.

I will try not to remember that Europe is finished,
That beautiful den of wolves, ancient and honored, down
   in the dust. I will watch the Pacific Ocean
Crawling under the mountain and the stars fly over,
   ancient, beautiful, offenseless, not honored.
   Why should I
Remember long misery and lamentation,
And the lost breath of the martyrs,
Thin smoke from dying altars,
And all the brave foolish boys and the women weeping?
Lie down dead bones. [*They resume cloaks and hoods.*]

THE LEADER.

I curse that night. I curse the bed and the lust. I wish my
   mother had died in that night
When she conceived me.

FRIEDENAU.   Leave those wandering voices:
   listen to victory.

THE LEADER.   Win or lose, I shall lose.
I'll pull some down with me. I would have been Europe's
   saviour: now come destruction. The beautiful
   cities
That watch themselves in their waters will be burnt rubble
And homeless mounds.

FRIEDENAU.   So feeble-hearted? This very

autumn you will storm Britain; you will sit in
London
Dictating terms. The endless vendetta of the English-
speakers will die of its hopelessness, and Pax
Germanica
Heal Europe's and the world's wounds. Hitler's name
Will take the sky of Caesar and Charlemagne.
Hail victory! [*He lifts his hand in salutation and goes out
into the night; resumes cloak and hood.*]

THE LEADER. I believe. I believe. I *will* believe.

[*The medium stretches, gasps and cries out, returning to
consciousness. In her struggle the basin of blood is thrown
over, and spills on the floor, to the Leader's feet.*]

THE LEADER [*recoiling*]. Ach! World over. . . . What a horror . . . [*He recovers self-control.*] Come. It is finished.
Give the woman five hundred marks.

WEISS. Sir, she always refuses presents.

STEINFURTH. She will take only the usual small fee.

[*They leave the cabin, behind the Leader. Outside, the
Maskers are standing rigidly still, against the curtain of
sea and sky.*]

FIRST MASKER.

Watch this man, half conscious of the future,
Pass to his tragic destiny.

[93]

THIRD.

The storm that broke the old rotten tree
Was justified by a sprouting acorn.

SECOND.

This man and the unconscious American
Are the two hands of the destroyer.

THIRD.

The storm that broke the old rotten tree
Was justified by a sprouting acorn.

THE LEADER [*he stops and turns, at the limit of the scene*].

Dogs! All that labor and faith
To die into mere bloody waste?

THIRD MASKER.

We must not wake him. Sleepwalker, dream,
While the storm roars in the tree.

THAT NOBLE FLOWER

Oh, noble, rich, glowing color of blood,
Too strong for the modern world to admire:
But Shakespeare's and Marlowe's audiences
Heard your hot red trumpet-call
At every turning of the steep tragedy;
And the end: the stage
Heaped with corpses and a few solemn words.

These wars, I suppose,
Flurry and drag, will drag on to such an end;
But who to say the great words? Churchill might . . . if
        Churchill
Could still be in power. We shall end meanly.

                              Dear God, remember us.
Give us a little nobility at last!
Make us worthy of the color of our wounds,
That high wild burning hue, brave as a trumpet's throat.
For now men fall in battle and that noble flower flowing
        from their bodies
Tells nothing except how beautiful they might have been.

[95]

I SHALL LAUGH
PURELY

1

TURN from that girl
Your fixed blue eyes.
Boy-slender she is,
And a face as beautiful as a hawk's face.
History passes like falling rocks.

I am old as a stone,
But she is beautiful.
War is coming.
All the fine boys will go off to war.
History passes like falling rocks.

Oh, that one's to marry
Another old man;
You won't be helped
When your tall sons go away to war.
History falls on your head like rocks.

[96]

Keep a straight mind
In the evil time.
In the mad-dog time
Why may not an old man run mad?
History falls like rocks in the dark,
All will be worse confounded soon.

2

Count the glories of this time,
Count that girl's beauty, then count England,
Bleeding, at bay, magnificent,
At last a lion,
For all will be worse confounded soon.

Count that girl's beauty, count the coast-range,
The steep rock that stops the Pacific,
Count the surf on its precipice,
The hawks in its air,
For all will be worse confounded soon.

Count its eagles and wild boars,
Count the great blue-black winter storms,
Heavy rain and the hurricane,

Get them by heart,
For all will be worse confounded soon.

Count no human thing but only
England's great fight and that girl's beauty,
History passes like falling
Rocks in the dark,
And all will be worse confounded soon.

3

But this, I steadily assure you, is not the world's end,
Nor even the end of a civilization. It is not so late as you
        think: give nature time.
These wars will end, and I shall lead a troupe of shaky old
        men through Europe and America,
Old drunkards, worn-out lechers; fallen dictators, cast
        kings, a disgraced president; some cashiered
        generals
And collapsed millionaires: we shall enact a play, I shall
        announce to the audience:
"All will be worse confounded soon."

We shall beware of wild dogs in Europe, and of the police
        in armed imperial America: —

[98]

For all that pain was mainly a shift of power: —we shall
       enact our play: "Oh Christian era,
Make a good end," but first I announce to our audiences:
       "This play is prophetic, it will be centuries.
This play does not represent the world's end,
But only the fall of a civilization. It is not so late as you
       think: give nature time."

In Europe we shall beware of starving dogs and political
       commissars, and of the police in America.
We shall rant on our makeshift stages in our cracked
       voices: "Oh Christian era,
Era of chivalry and the barbarians and the machines, era
       of science and the saints,
When you go down make a good sunset.
Never linger superfluous, old and holy and paralytic like
       India,
Go down in conclusive war and a great red sunset, great
       age go down,
For all will be worse confounded soon."
We shall tour to the last verge and the open Pacific, we
       shall sit on the yellow cliffs at Hurricane Point
And watch the centaurs come from the sea; their splayed
       hooves plunge and stutter on the tide-rocks,
       watch them swarm up,

[99]

The hairy and foamy flanks, the naked destructive
        shoulders, the brutal faces and the bent bows,
Horde after horde under the screaming gulls: my old men
        will cough in the fog and baa like sheep,
"Here comes the end of a civilization. Give nature time,"
And spit, and make lewd jokes. But I shall laugh purely,
Remembering what old enthusiast named a girl's beauty
        and England's battle
Among the lights of his time: she being by then a dyed
        hag, or more likely
One of those embalmer-fingered smiles in the subsoil; and
        England will be
Not admirable. I shall laugh purely, knowing the next age
Lives on not-human beauty, waiting on circumstance and
        its April, weaving its winter chrysalis;
Thin snow falls on historical rocks.

PRESCRIPTION OF PAINFUL ENDS

LUCRETIUS felt the change of the world in his time, the
       great republic riding to the height
Whence every road leads downward; Plato in his time
       watched Athens
Dance the down path. The future is a misted landscape,
       no man sees clearly, but at cyclic turns
There is a change felt in the rhythm of events, as when an
       exhausted horse
Falters and recovers, then the rhythm of the running hoof-
       beats is changed: he will run miles yet,
But he must fall: we have felt it again in our own life time,
       slip, shift and speed-up
In the gallop of the world; and now perceive that, come
       peace or war, the progress of Europe and
       America
Becomes a long process of deterioration—starred with
       famous Byzantiums and Alexandrias,
Surely—but downward. One desires at such times
To gather the insights of the age summit against future
       loss, against the narrowing mind and the tyrants,

The pedants, the mystagogues, the barbarians: one builds
      poems for treasuries, time-conscious poems:
      Lucretius
Sings his great theory of natural origins and of wise con-
      duct; Plato smiling carves dreams, bright cells
Of incorruptible wax to hive the Greek honey.
                                Our own
      time, much greater and far less fortunate,
Has acids for honey, and for fine dreams
The immense vulgarities of misapplied science and decay-
      ing Christianity: therefore one christens each
      poem, in dutiful
Hope of burning off at least the top layer of the time's
      uncleanness, from the acid-bottles.

FAITH

Ants, or wise bees, or a gang of wolves,
Work together by instinct, but man needs lies.
Man his admired and more complex mind
Needs lies to bind the body of his people together,
Make peace in the state and maintain power.
These lies are called a faith and their formulation
We call a creed, and the faithful flourish,
They conquer nature and their enemies, they win security.
Then proud and secure they will go awhoring
With that impractical luxury the love of truth,
That tries all things: alas the poor lies,
The faith like a morning mist burnt by the sun:
Thus the great wave of a civilization
Loses its forming soul, falls apart and founders.
Yet I believe that truth is more beautiful
Than all the lies, and God than all the false gods.
Then we must leave it to the humble and the ignorant
To invent the frame of faith that will form the future.
It was not for the Romans to produce Christ.
It was not for Lucretius to prophesy him, nor Pilate
To follow him. . . . Or could we change at last and
            choose truth?

THE EXCESSES OF GOD

Is it not by his high superfluousness we know
Our God? For to equal a need
Is natural, animal, mineral: but to fling
Rainbows over the rain
And beauty above the moon, and secret rainbows
On the domes of deep sea-shells,
And make the necessary embrace of breeding
Beautiful also as fire,
Not even the weeds to multiply without blossom
Nor the birds without music:
There is the great humaneness at the heart of things,
The extravagant kindness, the fountain
Humanity can understand, and would flow likewise
If power and desire were perch-mates.

THE SIRENS

PERHAPS we desire death: or why is poison so sweet?
Why do the little Sirens
Make kindlier music, for a man caught in the net of the
        world
Between news-cast and work-desk—
The little chirping Sirens, alcohol, amusement, opiates,
And carefully sterilized lust—
Than the angels of life? Really it is rather strange, for the
        angels
Have all the power on their side,
All the importance:—men turn away from them, pre-
        ferring their own
Vulgar inventions, the little
Trivial Sirens. Here is another sign that the age needs
        renewal.

BIRTHDAY

TIME to grow old;
Not to take in sail and be safe and temperate,
But drive the hull harder, drive the bows under.

Time to grow hard
And solitary: to a man past fifty the hot-eyed
Girls are still beautiful, but he is not.

Time to grow passionate.
Girls that take off their clothes, and the naked truth,
Have a quality in common: both are accessible.

Time to despise
Peace: that's under the prow: peace is an ocean
To conquer and traverse, and at last drown in.

Time who half wasted
The summer trade-wind should whistle for winter
      tempest,
And the tall blind cliffs of Terra Incognita.

MY DEAR LOVE

"Look up my dear at the dark
Constellations above."
"Dark stars under green sky.
I lie on my back and harken
To the music of the stars,
My dear love."

"You and I, my dear love,
Shall never die, never die."
"Not again, my dear love.
Lie on your back and hark
The music of moon and stars,
My dear love."

"Why do you never lie
On my breast, my dear love?"
"Oh, that was another sky.
Here, each of us on his own,
Each on his own back-bone,
My dear love."

"Is that the law of this land,
Each one of us on his own?"
"Oh, yes, we are underground
With the elves and fairies: lonely
Is the word in this country,
My dear love."

"What, a law in this land
That breast can never meet breast?"
"After while you will understand.
The mole is our moon, and worms
Are the stars we observe,
My dear love."

THE HOUSE DOG'S GRAVE

(Haig, an English bulldog)

I'VE changed my ways a little; I cannot now
Run with you in the evenings along the shore,
Except in a kind of dream; and you, if you dream a
> moment,
You see me there.

So leave awhile the paw-marks on the front door
Where I used to scratch to go out or in,
And you'd soon open; leave on the kitchen floor
The marks of my drinking-pan.

I cannot lie by your fire as I used to do
On the warm stone,
Nor at the foot of your bed; no, all the nights through
I lie alone.

But your kind thought has laid me less than six feet
Outside your window where firelight so often plays,

And where you sit to read—and I fear often grieving for
        me—
Every night your lamplight lies on my place.

You, man and woman, live so long, it is hard
To think of you ever dying.
A little dog would get tired, living so long.
I hope that when you are lying

Under the ground like me your lives will appear
As good and joyful as mine.
No, dears, that's too much hope: you are not so well
        cared for
As I have been.

And never have known the passionate undivided
Fidelities that I knew.
Your minds are perhaps too active, too many-sided . . . .
But to me you were true.

You were never masters, but friends. I was your friend.
I loved you well, and was loved. Deep love endures
To the end and far past the end. If this is my end,
I am not lonely. I am not afraid. I am still yours.

COME, LITTLE BIRDS

I PAID the woman what she asked, and followed her down
        to the water side, and her two sons
Came down behind us; one of them brought a spade, the
        other led the black calf and tied him up short
To a sycamore trunk over the stream-bank. It was near the
        foot of the mountain, where the Sur River
Pours from its gorge, foaming among great stones; and
        evening had come
But the light was still clear. The old woman brought us to
        a tongue of grassed land under the stream-bank;
One of her boys gathered dry sticks for a fire, the other
        cleared and repaired a short shallow trench
That scored the earth there; then they heaped up the sticks
        and made yellow flame, about ten feet from the
        trench
On the north side, right against the water; the woman sat
        opposite the fire and facing it, gazing northward,
Her back against a big stone.

[111]

             She closed her eyes and hummed
    tuneless music, nodding her vulturine head
To the dull rhythm; through which one heard the fire
    snoring and the river flowing, and the surf on
    the shore
Over the hill. After some time she widened her eyes, and
    their sight was rolled up
Under her forehead, I saw the firelight
Flicker on the blank whites; she raised her arms and cried
    out
In a loud voice. Instantly her two boys went up and
    fetched the black calf though he plunged and
    struggled.
They tied his hind feet with a tight knot, and passed the
    bight of the rope over a sycamore bough
That hung above the stream and the head of the trench;
    they tugged his hind feet up to it, so that he fell
On the knees of his forelegs over the trench-head. Then
    one of the two young men sheared the calf's
    throat
With a sharp knife, holding him by one ear, the other by
    an ear and the nostrils, and the blood spouted
Into the furrow. The woman, her body twitching
    convulsively, "Come, little birds."

She screamed through her tightened throat like a
      strangling person,
"Put on the life, here is the blood, come, you gray birds."

      By this time deep night had come,
And the fire down to red coals; there was a murmur along
      the stream-side as if a sea-wind were moving
Through the dark forest; then I saw dimly in the light of
      the coals the steam that climbed the cold air
From the hot blood and hung stagnant above the trench
Stirred, as if persons were stooping through it and stirring
      it; and distant whispers began to hiss in the
      trench,
And gray shapes moved. One said, wiry-thin: "Out of my
      way, you dregs." Another answered, "Stand back.
You've had your turn."

      These were no doubt the souls of
      the dead, that dark-eyed woman
Had promised would come and tell me what I had to
      know: they looked rather like starlight sheep,
That were driven through the dust all day and deep night
      has come, they huddle at a bend of the lane,
      scared by the dogs,

Gray and exhausted, and if one goes under the others
    trample him.

               One of the old woman's boys
Gradually revived the spent fire with dry leaves and twigs,
    so that the light increased imperceptibly,
Yet many of that whispering flock were frightened away.
    Those that remained, several still greedy
    cowered
Over the blood-trench, others erect wavered like long pale
    water-weeds; I went near them,
They sighed and whispered, leaning away from me like
    rooted water-weeds. I said, "if you are the souls
    of the dead,
And this old woman's trance and the warm blood make
    you able to answer—" and I was about to say,
"Then tell me what death is like: is it sleep or waking,
    captivity or freedom, dreams or reality?"—but
    they
Hearing my thought whispered, "We know, we know, we
    know," wavering like water-weeds; then one
    leaned toward me,
Saying, "Tell my mother." "What?" I said. "Tell her I
    was well enough

[114]

Before that old buzzard waked me. I died in the base-
  hospital—" Another of the forms crossed him
  and said
"God curse every man that makes war or plans it." (This
  was in nineteen twenty, about two years
After the Armistice.) "God curse every Congressman that
  voted it. God curse Wilson." His face like an axe
Passed between my eyes and the fire and he entered the
  darkness beyond the light-rim. I asked the other,
"What is your mother's name?" But he could not answer,
  but only stared at me. I said, "Does she live on
  the Coast
Or in Monterey?" He stared at me and struck his forehead
  and stood aside.

           Others came toward me, two of whom
Seemed to be women; but now I saw a known form, tall,
  gaunt, gray-haired, and the shoulders so stooped
They appeared like a hump; he leaned to the fire, warming
  his gray old hands. I avoided the other
Shapes of the dead and went to him; my heart was shaking
And my eyes wet. "Father," I said. He answered clearly,
  "Is that you, Robin?" I said, "Father,

Forgive me. I dishonored and wasted all your hopes of me,
      one by one; yet I loved you well."
He smiled calmly and answered, "I suppose hope is a folly.
      We often learn that
Before we die. We learn," he said, "nothing afterwards."
      Then I was silent, and breathed and asked,
"Is it a sleep?" "With a dream sometimes. But far too
      bloodless to grieve," he said, "or gladden the
      dreamer;
And soon, I conjecture, even this pin's weight and echo of
      consciousness that makes me speak to you
Will dissolve in the stream." He smiled and rubbed his
      gray hands together and said, "Amen. If you
      come
To Endor again I shall not be present." Then I wished to
      tell him
Our little news: that his name would continue in the
      world, for we had two sons now; and that my
      mother and my brother
Were well; and also the outcome of the great war, because
      he had died
In its fifth month. He was patient and let me speak, but
      clearly not cared at all.

                                Meanwhile the woman

Had been groaning in her trance; I noticed the shapes of
      the dead changed with her breathing: when she
      drew breath
They became stronger, when her breath was delayed they
      grew faint and vague. But now she became
      exhausted, her breathing
Was like a death-rattle, with terrifying pauses between the
      gasps. One of her boys ran to restore her;
The other heaped the fire high, and the pale dead
Were fleeing away; but a certain one of them came run-
      ning toward me, slender and naked, I saw the
      firelight
Glitter on her bare thighs; she said, "I am Tamar Cauldwell
      from Lobos: write my story. Tell them
I have my desire." She passed me and went like a lamp
      through the dark wood.
                    This was all. The young men
Carried their mother up to the cabin; I was left alone and
      stayed by the fire all night, studying
What I had heard and seen, until yellow dawn stood over
      the mountain.

                   This was all? I thought not.
I thought these decaying shadows and echoes of person-
      ality are only a by-play; they are not the spirit

That we see in one loved, or in saint or hero,

Shining through flesh. And I have seen it shine from a
       mountain through rock, and even from an old
       tree

Through the tough bark. The spirit (to call it so: what else
       could I call it?) is not a personal quality, and not

Mortal; it comes and goes, never dies. It is not to be found
       in death: dredge not the shadow-world. The
       dead

Have no news for us. We have for them, but they do not
       care. Peace to them.

CONTEMPLATION OF THE SWORD

(April, 1938)

REASON will not decide at last; the sword will decide.
The sword: an obsolete instrument of bronze or steel,
        formerly used to kill men, but here
In the sense of a symbol. The sword: that is: the storms
        and counter-storms of general destruction;
        killing of men,
Destruction of all goods and materials; massacre, more or
        less intentional, of children and women;
Destruction poured down from wings, the air made
        accomplice, the innocent air
Perverted into assassin and poisoner.

The sword: that is: treachery and cowardice, incredible
        baseness, incredible courage, loyalties,
        insanities.
The sword: weeping and despair, mass-enslavement, mass-
        torture, frustration of all the hopes
That starred man's forehead. Tyranny for freedom, horror
        for happiness, famine for bread, carrion for
        children.

Reason will not decide at last, the sword will decide.

Dear God, who are the whole splendor of things and the
        sacred stars, but also the cruelty and greed, the
        treacheries
And vileness, insanities and filth and anguish: now that
        this thing comes near us again I am finding it
        hard
To praise you with a whole heart.
                         I know what pain is, but
        pain can shine. I know what death is, I have
        sometimes
Longed for it. But cruelty and slavery and degradation,
        pestilence, filth, the pitifulness
Of men like little hurt birds and animals . . . if you were
        only
Waves beating rock, the wind and the iron-cored earth,
        the flaming insolent wildness of sun and stars,
With what a heart I could praise your beauty.
                           You will not repent,
        nor cancel life, nor free man from anguish
For many ages to come. You are the one that tortures him-
        self to discover himself: I am
One that watches you and discovers you, and praises you
        in little parables, idyl or tragedy, beautiful

[120]

Intolerable God.

          The sword: that is:

I have two sons whom I love. They are twins, they were
      born in nineteen sixteen, which seemed to us a
      dark year
Of a great war, and they are now of the age
That war prefers. The first-born is like his mother, he is so
      beautiful
That persons I hardly know have stopped me on the street
      to speak of the grave beauty of the boy's face.
The second-born has strength for his beauty; when he
      strips for swimming the hero shoulders and
      wrestler loins
Make him seem clothed. The sword: that is: loathsome
      disfigurements, blindness, mutilation, locked
      lips of boys
Too proud to scream.

          Reason will not decide at last: the
    sword will decide.

WATCH THE LIGHTS FADE

GRAY steel, cloud-shadow-stained,
The ocean takes the last lights of evening.
Loud is the voice and the foam lead-color,
And flood-tide devours the sands.

Here stand, like an old stone,
And watch the lights fade and hear the sea's voice.
Hate and despair take Europe and Asia,
And the sea-wind blows cold.

Night comes: night will claim all.
The world is not changed, only more naked:
The strong struggle for power, and the weak
Warm their poor hearts with hate.

Night comes: come into the house,
Try around the dial for a late news-cast.
These others are America's voices: naive and
Powerful, spurious, doom-touched.

How soon? Four years or forty?
Why should an old stone pick at the future?
Stand on your shore, old stone, be still while the
Sea-wind salts your head white.

NERVES

You have noticed the curious increasing exasperation
Of human nerves these late years? Not only in Europe,
Where reasons exist, but universal; a rope or a net
Is being hauled in, a tension screwed tighter;
Few minds now are quite sane; nearly every person
Seems to be listening for a crash, listening . . .
And *wishing* for it, with a kind of enraged
Sensibility.
          Or is it that we really feel
A gathering in the air of something that hates
Humanity; and in that storm-light see
Ourselves with too much pity and the others too clearly?

Well: this is February, nineteen-three-nine.
We count the months now; we shall count the days.
It seems time that we find something outside our
Own nerves to lean on.

THE SOUL'S DESERT

(August 30, 1939)

THEY are warming up the old horrors; and all that they say
       is echoes of echoes.
Beware of taking sides; only watch.
These are not criminals, nor hucksters and little journalists,
       but the governments
Of the great nations; men favorably
Representative of massed humanity. Observe them.
       Wrath and laughter
Are quite irrelevant. Clearly it is time
To become disillusioned, each person to enter his own
       soul's desert
And look for God—having seen man.

THE DAY IS A POEM

(September 19, 1939)

THIS morning Hitler spoke in Danzig, we heard his voice.
A man of genius: that is, of amazing
Ability, courage, devotion, cored on a sick child's soul,
Heard clearly through the dog wrath, a sick child
Wailing in Danzig; invoking destruction and wailing at it.
Here, the day was extremely hot; about noon
A south wind like a blast from hell's mouth spilled a slight
      rain
On the parched land, and at five a light earthquake
Danced the house, no harm done. Tonight I have been
      amusing myself
Watching the blood-red moon droop slowly
Into black sea through bursts of dry lightning and distant
      thunder.
Well: the day is a poem: but too much
Like one of Jeffers's, crusted with blood and barbaric
      omens,
Painful to excess, inhuman as a hawk's cry.

GREAT MEN

CONSIDER greatness.
A great man must have a following, whether he gain it
Like Roosevelt by grandiose good intentions, cajolery
And public funds, or like Hitler by fanatic
Patriotism, frank lies, genius and terror.
Without great following no greatness; it is ever the greedy
Flame on a wick dipped in the fat of millions;
No man standing alone has ever been great;
Except, most rarely, his will, passion or intellect
Have come to posthumous power, and the naked spirit
Picked up a crown.
                        Yes. Alas then, poor ghost,
Neitzsche or Jesus, hermit, martyr, starved prophet,
Were you honest while you lived? You are not now.
You have found your following and it corrupts you; all
            greatness
Involves betrayal, of the people by a man
Or of a man by the people. Better to have stood
Forever alone. Better been mute as a fish,
Or an old stone on the mountain, where no man comes

But only the wilderness-eyeing hawk with her catch
And feeds in peace, delicately, with little beakfuls,
While far down the long slope gleams the pale sea.

MOON AND FIVE PLANETS

FIVE planets and a brilliant young moon
Reach like a golden ladder from the saffron-lined sea-rim
High up the dark blue dome of heaven.
Today we saw the first flush of wild-flowers, glad was our
        hillside
With yellow violets and blue-eyed grass.
This beautiful day dying in such splendor is the tenth of
        March,
Nineteen forty; Finland today,
After all her winter valor and the great war in the snow,
Is beaten down by machines and multitude.
It will be long before the moon and five planets meet
        again;
And bitter things will have happened; not worse things.

BATTLE
(May 28, 1940)

FORESEEN for so many years: these evils, this monstrous
        violence, these massive agonies: no easier to
        bear.
We saw them with slow stone strides approach, everyone
        saw them; we closed our eyes against them, we
        looked
And they had come nearer. We ate and drank and slept,
        they came nearer. Sometimes we laughed, they
        were nearer. Now
They are here. And now a blind man foresees what follows
        them: degradation, famine, despair and so
        forth, and the
Epidemic manias: but not enough death to serve us, not
        enough death. It would be better for men
To be few and live far apart, where none could infect
        another; then slowly the sanity of field and
        mountain
And the cold ocean and glittering stars might enter their
        minds.

[130]

[BATTLE]

Another dream, another dream.

We shall have to accept certain limitations

In future, and abandon some humane dreams; only hard-
        minded, sleepless and realist can ride this rock-
        slide

To new fields down the dark mountain; and we shall have
        to perceive that these insanities are normal;

We shall have to perceive that battle is a burning flower or
        like a huge music, and the dive-bomber's
        screaming orgasm

As beautiful as other passions; and that death and life are
        not serious alternatives. One has known all these
        things

For many years: there is greater and darker to know

In the next hundred.

And why do you cry, my dear, why do you cry?

It is all in the whirling circles of time.

If millions are born millions will die;

In bed or in battle is no great matter

In the long orbits of time.

If England goes down and Germany up

The stronger dog will still be on top,

All in the turning of time.

If civilization goes down—that

[BATTLE]

Would be an event to contemplate.
It will not be in our time, alas, my dear,
It will not be in our time.

THE STARS GO OVER
THE LONELY OCEAN

UNHAPPY about some far off things
That are not my affair, wandering
Along the coast and up the lean ridges,
I saw in the evening
The stars go over the lonely ocean,
And a black-maned wild boar
Plowing with his snout on Mal Paso Mountain.

The old monster snuffled, "Here are sweet roots,
Fat grubs, slick beetles and sprouted acorns.
The best nation in Europe has fallen,
And that is Finland,
But the stars go over the lonely ocean,"
The old black-bristled boar,
Tearing the sod on Mal Paso Mountain.

"The world's in a bad way, my man,
And bound to be worse before it mends;
Better lie up in the mountain here

[133]

Four or five centuries,
While the stars go over the lonely ocean,"
Said the old father of wild pigs,
Plowing the fallow on Mal Paso Mountain.

"Keep clear of the dupes that talk democracy
And the dogs that talk revolution,
Drunk with talk, liars and believers.
I believe in my tusks.
Long live freedom and damn the ideologies,"
Said the gamey black-maned wild boar
Tusking the turf on Mal Paso Mountain.

FOR UNA

1

I BUILT her a tower when I was young—
Sometime she will die—
I built it with my hands, I hung
Stones in the sky.

Old but still strong I climb the stone—
Sometime she will die—
Climb the steep rough steps alone,
And weep in the sky.

Never weep, never weep.

2

Never be astonished, dear.
Expect change.
Nothing is strange.

[FOR UNA]

We have seen the human race
Capture all its dreams,
All except peace.

We have watched mankind like Christ
Toil up and up,
To be hanged at the top.

No longer envying the birds,
That ancient prayer for
Wings granted: therefore

The heavy sky over London,
Stallion-hoofed,
Falls on the roofs.

These are the falling years,
They will go deep,
Never weep, never weep.

With clear eyes explore the pit.
Watch the great fall
With religious awe.

3

It is not Europe alone that is falling
Into blood and fire.
Decline and fall have been dancing in all
        men's souls
For a long while.

Sometime at the last gasp comes peace
To every soul.
Never to mine until I find out and speak
The things that I know.

4

Tomorrow I will take up that heavy poem again
About Ferguson, deceived and jealous man
Who bawled for the truth, the truth, and failed to endure
Its first least gleam. That poem bores me, and I hope will
        bore
Any sweet soul that reads it, being some ways
My very self but mostly my antipodes;
But having waved the heavy artillery to fire
I must hammer on to an end.

Tonight, dear,
Let's forget all that, that and the war,
And enisle ourselves a little beyond time,
You with this Irish whiskey, I with red wine,
While the stars go over the sleepless ocean,
And sometime after midnight I'll pluck you a wreath
Of chosen ones; we'll talk about love and death,
Rock-solid themes, old and deep as the sea,
Admit nothing more timely, nothing less real
While the stars go over the timeless ocean,
And when they vanish we'll have spent the night well.

TWO CHRISTMAS-CARDS

1

THE seas netted with ambushes
And the sky falling:
Under that fiery rain
England is dying again,
Immortal and dying.
Look: vale beyond vale of vanished Englands.

The pilgrims to Canterbury
Ride by Kit's Coty House:
Someone before the Celt
Raised those great stones and felt
Securely immortal
Over vale beyond vale of vanished Englands.

Rain-loved Cumberland mountains
And the streams running down,
High sheep-runs by whom first claimed,
What poet in what language named
Glaramara
Before Wordsworth in his vanished England?

Lichen and stone the gables
Of Kelmscott watch the young Thames:
England dies in the storm,
Dies to survive, and form
Another and another
Of the veils under veils of the vanished Englands.

2

For an hour on Christmas eve
And again on the holy day,
Seek the magic of past time,
From this present turn away.
Dark though our day,
Light lies the snow on the hawthorn hedges
And the ox knelt down at midnight.

Only an hour, only an hour
From wars and confusions turn away
To the islands of old time
When the world was simple and gay,
Or so we say,
And light lay the snow on the green holly,
The tall oxen knelt at midnight.

Caesar and Herod shared the world,
Sorrow over Bethlehem lay,
Iron the empire, brutal the time,
Dark was that first Christmas day,
Dark was that day,
Light lay the snow on the mistletoe berries
And the ox knelt down at midnight.

DRUNKEN CHARLIE

(A person in the poem called "Give Your Heart
to the Hawks")

1

I AM dancing on the silver beach,
The bright moon is in my reach,
Willing girl with skin of pearl,
But nobody knows the turns of the world,
I won't touch her, for the tides
Run along her tender sides
Like foaming hounds,
And oh the long water might wash me under.

I am a fisherman by trade,
And a drunkard as they say.
I dance alone to my own song,
Doctor says I won't live long,
Bowels blench and kidneys fret,
Doctor, I'll live ten years yet,
Drinking and dancing,
Unless the long water should wash me under.

Life is short but I have seen
The bitter ends of better men,
I have seen Michael and Lance Fraser
And Bruce Ferguson swim to heaven,
Long naked ghosts gleaming like fishes,
Dead men walk on the hills like torches,
Why should we cry for them?
Some night or some morning we all wash under.

Once I cried and that's enough.
I drew a girl into my skiff,
A bright girl from the blue wave,
She had not been dead three days.
I combed her hair and kissed her feet,
She was so quiet and so sweet,
I cried my heart out,
And wished the long water would wash me under.

I am by trade a hunter of fishes,
And a drunkard by conviction.
I've a kettle hid in a rift
Under the great lifting cliff
That I think might trouble the wise
If they smelled its mysteries.
Holy King Solomon,
Here is a magic that puts yours under.

From potatoes or common corn
I can make a God be born.
I spent a year in the county jail
For making God enter a pail
Through a coil of copper tube:
Is that worse than a virgin's womb?
Fill me with God,
And the water may wash this old carcass under.

2

Where did that drowned girl voyage from?
Why did she die?
On the blue water and foam
Where did that girl voyage from?
I never think but I cry.

She had a lover, I believe,
Why did she die?
He was false or else a thief,
She had a lover, I believe.
It is better to drink than to cry.

She was too kind, they were too merry,
Why did she die?
She was too kind, they were too merry.

Or was it death that swelled her belly?
I never think but I cry.

She wavered up through the green water
Like a moth flying.
She came to my boat on the blue water
As if she had been my own daughter.
Drinking's better than crying
But oh, child, why?
Said pickled in whiskey to pickled in brine.

3

She answered me, or did I dream?
She lay so passive and so sweet
In the stern of the boat,
And her body sang like a lark:
April, oh April.

I had a lover I believe
And he was neither false nor a thief,
He was torn by sea-lions' teeth
In the bitter month of April.

I know a beach where sea-lions drag
Their boat-hull bodies up the strand,

No one comes there, dear lover,
And the great cliff hangs over.
April, oh April.

My brothers they have eyes like hawks,
They ride all day watching the calves;
Or their hounds would find your tracks
In the bitter month of April.

He came to me under the cliff
And I could never have enough.
He came to me in March
And my soul was parched
For April, oh April.

The long sea-lions lie on the strand,
I used to stroke them with my hand,
How could I know that they turn bad
In the bitter month of April?

There was one that I loved well,
I would have trusted him with all,
He watched once while my dear
And I did the secret thing.
But not in April.

[DRUNKEN CHARLIE]

In April they began to stir,
Their long sea-women came ashore,
I never cared how much they roared
In the bitter month of April.

If their loves came, why should not mine?
I watched them crawl up from the brine,
I loved to watch them come
Out of the sea foam

In April, oh April.

They used to fight, I hated that.
Sometimes the blood ran on the sand.
Yet I could stroke them with my hand
Even in the month of April.

These northern sea-lions they are longer
Than the length of two men, and stronger
Than all but the killer whale:
I never knew that I cared.
April, oh April.

My love came striding up the strand,
He touched the beast, it caught his hand,

How could we know that they turn bad
In the bitter month of April?

Oh red thing writhing on the sand
How could we know when they turn bad?
This was their breeding-season,
Cruelty was out of prison.
April, oh April.

4

She lay in the stern of the boat,
And her body sang like a lark:
I curse the war-makers, I curse
Those that run to the ends of the earth
To exalt a system or save
A foreign power or foreign trade.

My boy was killed by a sea-lion,
And that was cruel but it was clean.
There are men plotting to kill
A million boys for a dead dream.

Oh my dear, there are some things
That are well worth fighting for.
Fight to save a sea-gull's wings:
That would be a sacred war.

SHINE, EMPIRE

POWERFUL and armed, neutral in the midst of madness,
      we might have held the whole world's balance
      and stood
Like a mountain in a wind. We were misled and took sides.
      We have chosen to share the crime and the
      punishment.

Perhaps justly, being part of Europe. Three thousand
      miles of ocean would hardly wash out the stains
Of all that mish-mash, blood, language, religion, snobbery.
      Three thousand miles in a ship would not make
      Americans.

I have often in weak moments thought of this people as
      something higher than the natural run of the
      earth.
I was quite wrong; we are lower. We are the people who
      hope to win wars with money as we win elections.

Hate no one. Roosevelt's intentions were good, and Hitler
        is a patriot. They have split the planet into two
        millstones
That will grind small and bloody; but still let us keep some
        dignity, these days are tragic, and fight without
        hating.

It is war, and no man can see an end of it. We must put
        freedom away and stiffen into bitter empire.
All Europe was hardly worth the precarious freedom of
        one of our states: what will her ashes fetch?

If I were hunting in the Ventana canyons again with my
        strong sons, and to sleep under stars,
I should be happy again. It is not time for happiness.
        Happy the blind, the witless, the dead.

Now, thoroughly compromised, we aim at world rule, like
        Assyria, Rome, Britain, Germany, to inherit
        those hordes
Of guilt and doom. I am American, what can I say but
        again, "Shine, perishing republic?" . . . Shine,
        empire.

THE BLOODY SIRE

It is not bad. Let them play.
Let the guns bark and the bombing-plane
Speak his prodigious blasphemies.
It is not bad, it is high time,
Stark violence is still the sire of all the world's values.

What but the wolf's tooth whittled so fine
The fleet limbs of the antelope?
What but fear winged the birds, and hunger
Jeweled with such eyes the great goshawk's head?
Violence has been the sire of all the world's values.

Who would remember Helen's face
Lacking the terrible halo of spears?
Who formed Christ but Herod and Caesar,
The cruel and bloody victories of Caesar?
Violence, the bloody sire of all the world's values.

Never weep, let them play,
Old violence is not too old to beget new values.

BE ANGRY AT THE SUN

THAT public men publish falsehoods
Is nothing new. That America must accept
Like the historical republics corruption and empire
Has been known for years.

Be angry at the sun for setting
If these things anger you. Watch the wheel slope
       and turn,
They are all bound on the wheel, these people,
       those warriors,
This republic, Europe, Asia.

Observe them gesticulating,
Observe them going down. The gang serves lies,
       the passionate
Man plays his part; the cold passion for truth
Hunts in no pack.

You are not Catullus, you know,
To lampoon these crude sketches of Caesar. You
       are far

From Dante's feet, but even farther from his dirty
Political hatreds.

Let boys want pleasure, and men
Struggle for power, and women perhaps for fame,
And the servile to serve a Leader and the dupes
        to be duped.
Yours is not theirs.

INDEX OF FIRST LINES